STUDYING MEDIA

Diar.

STUDYING MEDIA

Problems of Theory and Method

———◦◦———

John Corner

EDINBURGH
University Press

© John Corner, 1998

Edinburgh University Press
22 George Square, Edinburgh

Typeset in Palatino Light
by Pioneer Associates, Perthshire, and
printed and bound in Great Britain by
The Cromwell Press, Trowbridge, Wilts

A CIP record for this book is available from the
British Library

ISBN 0 7486 1067 7

The right of John Corner to be identified as
author of this work has been asserted in
accordance with the Copyright, Designs and
Patents Act 1988.

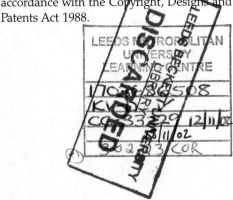

CONTENTS

ACKNOWLEDGEMENTS

I would like to acknowledge publishers' permission to reprint material as follows: Edward Arnold/Hodder and Stoughton Educational for 'Criticism as Sociology' from J. Hawthorn (ed.) *Criticism and Critical Theory*, 1984, 29–41 and for 'Meaning, Genre and Context' from J. Curran and M. Gurevitch (eds) *Mass Media and Society*, 1991, 267–84; Sage Publications Ltd for 'Codes and Cultural Analysis' from *Media, Culture and Society* 2.1. 1980, 73–86, 'Debating Culture' from *Media, Culture and Society* 16.1. 1994, 141–8 and 'Television in Theory' from *Media, Culture and Society* 19.2. 1997, 247–62; Addison Wesley Longman for 'Why Study Media Form' from A. Briggs and P. Cobley (eds) *The Media: An Introduction*, 1997, 238–49; Oxford University Press for 'Mass in Communication Research' from *Journal of Communication* 19.1. 1979, 26–32, 'Presumption as Theory' from *Screen* 33.1. 1992, 97–102 and 'Media Studies and the Knowledge Problem' from *Screen* 36.2. 1995, 145–55. In each case I am the sole author.

In bringing together material from two decades of work in the field I incur a range of debts too extensive for specific acknowledgement. I would particularly like to thank my Liverpool colleagues, past and present, for the benefits of their conversation and the joint teaching and research which I have undertaken with them.

Finally, I would like to thank Jackie Jones of Edinburgh University Press for encouraging me to put together this collection and reflect further on the general development of the field since the 1970s.

John Corner

Chapter 1

INTRODUCTION
The Formation of a Field

What perspectives can we best use to understand the media? In what measures and combinations might we mix the established ideas of Arts and Social Science Scholarship? Should we seek an interdisciplinary integration or a multidisciplinary approach which acknowledges the conventional discipline boundaries? What theories and concepts seem most useful for development and what most open to question? How can we relate theory to analysis and what different kinds of methodological problem does analysis of the various dimensions of media and mediation pose? Perhaps most importantly of all, what are the aims of media study, what kinds of knowledge do we hope to produce and for what purpose?

This collection contains nine essays which I have written on such questions. The questions concern problems of a type broadly familiar in many other areas of inquiry but they also concern problems quite distinctive to the character of media study and its institutionalisation as a field for research and teaching. The essays cover a twenty-year span, the first being published in 1979. They were all stimulated by my experience of working within the project of British 'Communication Studies', and specifically within the media focus of this project, from the mid-1970s. As a result, there is often a strong national character to my argument and ideas, although they are also informed by the international development of the field, relating back to earlier phases of study in the United States but also across to concurrent work both in North America, continental Europe and Scandinavia. Like many others, I have found study of the media to connect intellectual imagination and exploratory scholarship to a sense of deep changes in

1

the organisation of society and culture in a very exciting way. It is not surprising that the academic response to such a profound and relatively swift pattern of change – pushing and pulling at conventional ways of understanding art and society, public and private, the relation of individual to group and the co-ordinates of place and time – has produced its fair crop of problems.

In this introduction, I want to outline some of the history of 'Media Studies' as a focus for higher education teaching and academic research in Britain. This history is both an intellectual history – the development of particular concerns, interests and ideas across disciplines – and an institutional history – the development of certain kinds of course, with their distinctive curricula, reading lists and staff teams as well as the emergence of academic communities at the level of the conference, the national association and the journal readership. Having provided a historical sketch, I shall then move on to a second stage of the chapter and identify some principal strands and issues contributing to the identity of the field in the late 1990s. Finally, I shall briefly examine a number of points of challenge for Media Studies in the future and assess the extent to which it is currently responding to these. I hope all this will provide a grounded story about Media Studies and a map upon which to locate the more detailed appraisals and arguments of subsequent chapters.

INSTITUTION AND FIELD

In the 1960s, strands of work on aspects of public communication were to be found in many disciplines, including importantly a 'sociology of mass communication' to which British or British-based academics such as Jay Blumler, Phillip Elliott, James Halloran, Denis McQuail and Jeremy Tunstall were contributing. The Leicester University Centre for Mass Communication Research had opened in 1966 and as well as carrying out a number of funded studies it had attracted postgraduate students and research assistants, many of whose work would prove influential in the later expansion of the area as a focus for degree programmes. In 1963, the Centre for Contemporary Cultural Studies had started at Birmingham, directed by Richard Hoggart with, quite soon afterwards, the assistance of Stuart Hall, and this quickly worked to consolidate some of the thinking about media and culture coming from scholars of English Literature, notably Hoggart's own writings on class and culture and the influential, theoretical/historical commentaries of Raymond Williams. Behind both writers lay the distinctively British strand of largely pessimistic commentary, running through from such earlier literary critics as Matthew Arnold, T. S. Eliot and F. R. Leavis, about art, value and social change. Leavis (1930) was particularly influential as a point of reference for development, or for rebuttal, in the early phases of Cultural Studies thinking. The Centre added to this literary base by engaging with a range of work in sociology and social psychology (for instance, that of Peter Berger and Erving Goffman) and, increasingly, by framing its inquiries within the terms of a structuralist Marxism derived largely, though not without criticism and modification, from the writings on ideology and the social formation of Louis Althusser. The structuralist anthropology of Lévi-Strauss and the structuralist writings on signs of Roland Barthes and Umberto Eco provided a source of more specific ideas about how the 'messages' of the mass media were active within the culture and of significance in the exercising of power and the maintenance of inequality. Later, the writings of Antonio Gramsci and Michel Foucault were major influences, as were many currents of feminist thinking.

The emphasis of the Birmingham Centre on questions of symbolic organisation and symbolic process (extending well beyond attention to the media although public mediation remained at the core of their published studies) often contrasted with the emphasis of the Leicester Centre on a more traditional sociological agenda of 'influence and effects', institutional organisation and production processes. When both Centres became notable for their Marxist or Marxian work, the contrast was between the 'critical cultural theory and analysis' of Birmingham, strongly inclined towards textual analysis as far as media research was concerned, and the 'political economy' perspectives of Leicester, on the whole not so much interested in language, image and symbolic organisation as in what were seen to be their economic, institutional and processual determinants.

It is possible to overstate the intellectual division between the two Centres and thereby to attribute degrees of naivety or ignorance to each in a distorting and insulting way. Nevertheless, there is a real sense in which Birmingham and Leicester acted as twin 'nodes', sometimes complementary but more often conflicting, in the development and institutionalisation of communication studies and then media studies which began in the early 1970s. What both reflected though, was the way in which British political and public life and British popular culture had now become impossible to address without a better and more systematic understanding of media systems, practices and processes. The prompt for investigation was in both cases a sense of anxiety, a concern about the consequences of the media within the political and cultural contexts of a changing Britain. And in both cases the nature of the response led away from the 'mainstream' of, respectively, Arts or Social Science inquiry towards a more interdisciplinary and politically radical approach.

If the developing, post-war interest in mass communication systems and their influence and in the changing character of popular culture was the primary factor in the intellectual formation of 'Communication Studies', there is also a level of institutional formation which needs to be considered too. In the early 1970s, British Higher Education was undergoing a major expansion as institutions, often former Technical Colleges, came together with the old Teacher Training Colleges and Colleges of Art to form the 'Polytechnics'. The mergings and amalgamations involved in the development of Polytechnics were sometimes rapidly achieved and sometimes took several years of growth. However, whatever the route taken, a need for extensive degree-level course development to redeploy a new, large and various staffing base and to attract a new kind of student was widely felt.

It was a financial imperative that attractive courses be offered as quickly as possible. Interdisciplinarity, Multidisciplinarity and 'Combined' programmes (rather than the traditional University 'single honours' model) were desirable because of the way they drew effectively on mixed teaching expertise and could absorb some of the oddities of balance between specialisms which the formative mergers and voluntary redundancies had created. Programmes which were also able to project themselves as in some way 'applied' rather than 'pure' studies had the added advantage of appearing to fulfil the Polytechnic mission as it was formulated at this stage of their development; a policy of providing an education 'equal to but different from' that of the University sector. 'Communication Studies' was an attractive route for development on both counts. A three-year programme of work around 'communication' could be delivered by a disparate group of Arts and Social Science staff, only a small core group of whom required specialist media interests or knowledge of that specific intellectual context surrounding analysis of the media within British culture which I noted above. Such programmes were 'applied' in the sense that they could be seen as a response to the increasing scale and diversity of the media industries and the growing number of jobs broadly in the 'communications' field, including those in public relations and personnel management. They were not 'vocational' courses in the direct sense of training students in specific professional tasks for, in most cases, there was no staff expertise to make this a significant part of a degree programme.

From the early 1970s onwards, the CNAA (Council for National Academic Awards) established a panel for 'Communication Studies' which had the task of reviewing course proposals and visiting institutions in order to validate (or not) particular programmes of study. In general, it operated with a very generous perspective on what the label might mean in any given institutional setting. The fact that Schools of Communication, Communications Associations and a journals literature using the designation 'Communication' had been established in United States academia for some time offset any sense of an entirely new venture. Professor Jay Blumler, the first chairman of the CNAA's panel, was fully familiar with the US tradition and a major figure within it, although there was no attempt to impose the distinctive features of the American development (Departments of Journalism, Departments of Speech, a strong behavioural science interest in interpersonal communication) upon a situation which clearly had its own quite distinctive origins and aspirations. The CNAA's criteria were based less on a sense of the 'ideal' combination of parts than on the competence of staff to teach the individual elements, the intellectual quality of these elements and the general soundness of provision for resources, teaching and assessment.

For instance, the course which I had close experience of at this time was the one developed at Sunderland University (then Sunderland Polytechnic) from 1976. As in many institutions, this 'specialist' programme was only put forward after a broader degree programme (Combined Studies, Arts and Social Sciences, in our case) had already been validated and the institution was therefore seen as able to operate at degree level in contributory disciplines. The Sunderland scheme placed its core media courses in the second and third years, following a first year which drew substantially on work in Sociology, Psychology, Linguistics and Literary and Art criticism to provide a broad foundational level. This was 'multidisciplinary' rather than 'interdisciplinary' in that it recognised the specific conceptual and methodological identity of contributing disciplines. In the second and third years, many of the course units, particularly the options, were defined by substantive topic (e.g. audience research, the British press, society and culture in the 1930s, popular culture) and adopted an interdisciplinary approach in which an eclectic mix of ideas and methods was used with less concern for the marking of different disciplinary inputs. Given the scattered, various literature on British media, this approach was virtually a necessity in offering any kind of comprehensive attention to institutions, practices, forms and audiences.

The Sunderland course also allowed for options outside of the media area however (for instance, in Art history, Literature and even Philosophy). It was able to offer a 'rationale' for itself (a necessary element of the course proposal document) at the very broad and *academic* level of the importance of the study of meaning, information and representation across a number of disciplines pursuing broadly convergent lines of inquiry. This was a self-consciously loose identity (in essence, such courses were a kind of 'combined honours' programme, although with a tighter degree of route coherence than would normally be imposed on students following such a course). As I have observed, their 'applied' character was often worn lightly, however much mention of the growth of the communications industry figured in course documents and publicity. In the first year of recruitment at Sunderland, the brochure designed for applicants was careful to stress the academic character of the programme and the lack of any kind of career promise directly consequent upon the final qualification.

Jay Blumler, writing in 1977, noted the degree of 'curricular solipsism' which prevailed as a result of different institutional staffing resources as well as different ideas about what was most interesting and where the most significant interdisciplinary connections lay. It is relevant for my further discussion of vocationalism that he also remarked how at this stage 'the courses that have been developed are ambitious, exciting and more theoretically than practically or vocationally oriented' (Blumler, 1977: 38).

At the time of the development of the Sunderland course, the programme at Sheffield Polytechnic (now Sheffield Hallam University) was the one to which we most often referred. Although there can be dispute about which undergraduate course was the first one in the area (some college courses were validated by a parent university rather than the CNAA, and there were many courses in which work on Communications was only a component, if sometimes the major one), the course at Sheffield has some claim to this status nationally. From the Sunderland perspective, the Sheffield programme was a little heavy on the literary side, with a strong representation of English staff. The Sunderland programme attempted to develop a stronger complementary emphasis on visual communication through work on art, photography and film. Such variations were seen as a matter of choice and, to some extent, as I have suggested, a matter of necessity in relation to staffing and resources.

However, even as the Sunderland course was in its early stages of refinement, two other models of degree work in the area had achieved validation. At the Polytechnic of Central London (now the University of Westminster) a BA course in 'Media Studies' was offered, drawing extensively on media professional skills and having half of its programme given over to varieties of practical training. Such a semi-vocational programme consequently drew a much tighter focus around the media than the Communication courses, although one could argue that it thereby provided students with a narrower academic experience. Meanwhile, at Portsmouth Polytechnic (now the University of Portsmouth) a BA course in 'Cultural Studies' had been devised. Here, the development was from an imaginative mixing of history and literary studies, producing a course which considered the media but situated them only as one object of study among a number of cultural forms and cultural settings. The Portsmouth model was, unsurprisingly, greatly influenced by the work of the Birmingham Centre.

Neither the 'Media Studies' nor the 'Cultural Studies' model lent themselves to easy reproduction elsewhere at this stage, given the technical resources and/or levels of staff specialism they required (the Polytechnic of Central London benefited from its proximity to major media production). There was also a widespread feeling that the 'Cultural Studies' perspective, although intellectually fertile, was too demandingly abstract and critique-driven to act satisfactorily as the

designator of undergraduate studies. It signalled not so much a substantive field of inquiry as a very specific intellectual problematic about
meaning, values and power under circumstances of social change,
marking a route from the conservativism of Leavisian literary criticism
to the radical critiques of Marxist cultural theory (the ambivalent,
quasi-celebratory tones of the postmodern approach were not then
apparent).

Subsequent developments nevertheless saw these two models
gradually become the preferred way of offering undergraduate studies
in the area, as against the initial, broad Communication Studies
approach. This shift was in part aided by a softening and expansion of
Cultural Studies as a category – the politicised theoretical concerns of
the Birmingham Centre giving way to a more descriptive and inclusive
usage, drawing in a number of areas of inquiry and, indeed, of arts
performance, where questions of social relationships and cultural value
had become more directly raised. Increasingly, Cultural Studies
became a *post-facto* term of institutional convenience to describe an
Arts-based mix of studies in which issues of contemporary social
change, including those surrounding the media, figured prominently.

Media Studies, meanwhile, emerged from the more comprehensive
intellectual framework of Cultural Studies and the more comprehensive pedagogic precedent of Communication Studies to establish itself
as what, by the early 1990s, was the primary designator – a process
which, as I shall suggest below, was very much to do with the
strengthening of its vocational promise.

These various strands of development, running throughout the
1970s, led to a situation in which, by the end of the decade, a new
subject group around study of media had been formed among Higher
Education teachers, chiefly those in the Polytechnics. Some of these
teachers were redeployed from earlier duties in Sociology, Psychology
and Literature, while some continued to work in traditional discipline
fields as well as within the interdisciplinary media programmes of the
new courses. An influential few were appointed directly from the
research centres themselves (Birmingham and Leicester particularly,
but also other University departments) to form a specialist core on the
new degrees. Few of the new programmes could be launched without
at least a modest investment in such appointments.

The formation of this subject group produced changes in the

academic subculture. There was a growth in conferences on media, in publications specialising in media research and commentary, and in associations and networks committed to discussing problems in teaching and research. Established journals like the British Film Institute's *Screen* and *Screen Education*, which were initially focused on film, started to reflect the broader terms of media interest (particularly the latter title), whilst *Media, Culture and Society* was launched in 1979 from a base in what was then a School of Communications (at the Polytechnic of Central London) offering a Media Studies course.

It is useful to note two further points about these institutional developments. Firstly, a tension between broadly Arts and broadly Social Scientific approaches was evident in most programmes in one form or other. In the more eclectic 'Communications' models, it was quite decisive from which primary perspective the core media units were taught. This tension was overlaid and perhaps compounded by the way in which Marxist critical theory, with its emphasis on the critique of ideology, had become central both to a strong strand of Literary Criticism and to much work in Cultural Studies. Questions about the aims, guiding concepts and methodological protocols of study were often answered very differently across the various parts of a programme, although the best courses managed to incorporate a good level of thoughtful pluralism and perspectival debate into their schemes.

Secondly, what I have termed the 'vocational promise' of work in this area remained a difficulty in the emergence of course identity. It was not easily neglectable, if only because it was clear that a primary reason for many school-leavers applying for these new courses was an interest in getting jobs in the media industry. However much the idea that the courses were somehow direct pathways to such jobs was denied by responsible course teams, in a situation where many institutions were only just beginning to establish themselves as having degree-level opportunities it would have been dangerous to have denied completely the vocational allure. Those few Cultural Studies programmes which had developed suffered from it least, since their structure and approach was so clearly intellectualist. 'Film Studies' also remained relatively untroubled by it, usually combining with English or Drama to produce courses legitimated within the established terms of Arts scholarship, terms much more extendable to film (with its marked authorialism and traditions of European 'seriousness') than to television. Media Studies programmes variously embraced it, depending on their resources and staff skills. I noted above that to offer an entire BA course on 'Media' seemed to demand a good measure of practical work and professional-level training (certainly the view taken by the CNAA, which had then to liaise with the different professional bodies concerned with accreditation and standards). This was true even if 'media' included an element of Film Studies and perhaps study of popular music, which it sometimes did but frequently did not. Meanwhile, Communication Studies programmes continued to work with a 'soft vocational' idea, indicating indirect benefits in the nature of course content and in the inclusion of a number of more practical activities, serving to introduce media skills at 'workshop' levels rather than at a level appropriate to pre-professional training.

On many courses, however, questions of just *how much* practical work and of *what kind* became pressing, with a slow drift towards including more non-academic options if only as a result of student expectations and enthusiasms. By the mid-1980s, it was Media Studies, involving an element of training, rather than Communication Studies, with perhaps only basic practical exercises, which was dominant. A certain vocationalisation of the field had occurred, making things awkward for courses which were unwilling, or whose staff felt unable, to respond. Yet the continuing attitude of the media industries towards undergraduate work in this area was lukewarm at best. Both in television production and in print and broadcast journalism, the industry preferred to make its own arrangements for training. In such a competitive field, it was clearly not going to privilege 'Media' or 'Communication' students over the full range of graduate talent when it came to recruitment. Indeed, there was an acute problem of professional and intellectual credibility to be overcome here rather than an advantage to be secured. As I shall suggest later, there still is – and this may turn out to be the most pressing problem for British Media Studies, as a field of teaching, in the future.

It is rather curious that at about the same time as the more vocationalist version of Media Studies was becoming established, undergraduate courses in the area started to be offered in the older University (as distinct from the Polytechnic) sector. Some of these courses (as at Glasgow, Warwick and Kent, for example) developed from an earlier teaching base in Film Studies, others grew from older research centres (like Birmingham, Leeds, Leicester and Liverpool) while still others were created quite rapidly by the appointment of new staff (Goldsmith's College, London, Loughborough, Stirling and Sussex are various examples of this).

The emergence of Media Studies in the more established institutions, often leading to the development of departments of 'media and communication', 'film and media', 'media and cultural studies', etc. had two direct consequences. Firstly, it made the recruitment of the better qualified school-leavers more difficult for the Polytechnics, because the option of studying the media at a University was often very attractive (the giving of University title and status to the Polytechnics in the 1990s eased this problem but only marginally, since a division between the 'old' and the 'new' parts of the sector remained strongly in the minds of many applicants, schoolteachers, parents and employers).

Secondly, it had some countering effect on the idea that studying the media was essentially a second-rate option, not to be compared at all with work in the traditional disciplines. By recruiting students with high A level grades, who often combined their media work with traditional Arts and Social Sciences studies and frequently achieved high final awards across both parts of their programme, the Universities strengthened the legitimacy of the area and made it a more acceptable choice in the eyes of schools considering the future of their best pupils. However, this effect has to be set against the fact that general prejudice against Media Studies, and particularly against what was perceived as its pseudo-vocational character, was to heighten not diminish in the course of the 1980s and 1990s and that little by way of a really effective defence of the area's academic value was mounted. It may be that the sheer scale of applications for media-related courses, leading to the most popular institutions having many times more applicants than they had places, caused a degree of 'boom' complacency in the field and a neglect of the requirement to argue and lobby against developing prejudice both within and without the educational establishment.

INTELLECTUAL CONSTITUENTS OF 'MEDIA STUDIES'

I want now to drop down to a closer level of commentary and to identify three important elements in development. I do this fully aware of the fact that a great variety of approaches and mixes were to be found from the mid-1970s onwards and that any suggestion of one neat model falsifies the intellectual vitality and ferment of the area at the time. Nevertheless, a dominant tendency there certainly was and it was influential in shaping the identity of the field at national level. It seems to me that a consideration of three distinct but related perspectives – Marxist, Linguistic and Ethnographic – gets us close to many important formative factors, albeit at the cost of some simplification.

a) Marxism

The influence of Marxist ideas on a range of humanities and social science thinking is clear, with a strengthening of the impact upon British thinking from the 1960s onwards. The post-1960s growth is in large measure a response to the varieties of 'neo-marxist' thinking in Europe – a rediscovery of the 1930s Frankfurt School writers on 'critical social theory' and the taking up of themes from the radical philosophers and political and cultural theorists working from within the social changes and social movements of the 1960s (Herbert Marcuse, Hans Magnus Enzensberger, Pierre Bourdieu and Louis Althusser are important and very different examples, later to be joined by Jurgen Habermas, after the belated translation of his work into English and by the rediscovery of Antonio Gramsci, again following the availability of translations).

For many people researching and teaching about media, Marxist concepts engaged illuminatingly with two rather different but large questions concerning public communications. Firstly, the question of the relation between economic power and political and cultural power. The factors of capital accumulation, the maximisation of profit and the 'commodification' (with resultant inequalities) of the media realm seemed coherently addressable from within this perspective.

Secondly, the question of the power of the media, their influence over consciousness and yet their apparent ability to naturalise both their visual and verbal accounts and their entertainments in such a way as to seem above any partisanship or partiality, raised questions about 'ideology'. 'Ideology' became from the 1960s one of the most intensively theorised and debated terms in the humanities and social science literatures. Questions about its epistemological and discursive character, about the extent and nature of its dominance and about the processes of its reproduction were on the agenda of many sub-areas of inquiry. Conference papers, journal articles and books reflected this. Media analysis was always likely to give the ideology question special attention since it was the new systems of public communications (particularly television) which were often seen to be the primary agents of ideological management. This contrasted, for instance, with the 'ideology debate' in literary studies, where questions were most often posed about how an ideologically-aware analysis might reveal the relations between texts and political contexts *in the past*.

The literary emphasis was therefore historiographic rather than being directly a matter of contemporary, political commentary, even allowing for the significance of the past for the present. The most developed form in which the 'ideology' question was posed, that of Marxist structuralism as exemplified in the writings of Louis Althusser (particularly 1971), quite quickly became established as canonical within the new field, both in teaching and in research. This influence was part of a more general structuralist influence, most notably that of a Semiotic analysis of images and of language, coming through from writings such as those of Roland Barthes (for example, 1977) and Umberto Eco (for instance, 1972), which themselves referred back to the posthumously published writings of the linguist Ferdinand de Saussure (1959). To tremendous enthusiasm and accompanied by varieties of intellectual publicity from publishers and journals, the 'Marxist–structuralist' focus became the guiding paradigm in the broad sector, in different ratios of mix (structuralism was often professed more strongly than Marxism by some writers, particularly those within Literary and Film Studies). Such an assessment perhaps understates the degree of intellectual disquiet which the perspective caused among a number of media researchers and the extent to which other-minded scholars and teachers continued to work from within the perspectives of, for instance, classical sociology and social psychology. However, my intention here is to sketch the broad tendencies which would prove defining for the national field as a whole, and 'Marxist–structuralism' was undoubtedly one of these. As I suggest later, its hold, however residual, continues to prove a difficulty for development and revision within the subject area.

It is worth noting that the other broad way of applying Marxist analysis to the media, the study of its 'political economy', mentioned above, did not influence the research and teaching agenda in anything like the same way. Part of the reason for this is perhaps that most of the new tendencies were converging around symbolic forms, discourse and language as the focal area for development. Teaching around questions of 'meaning' was seen to be a more successful way of providing attractive courses which drew on a number of intellectual traditions. Focusing on questions of economics and institutional organisation was not so directly compatible with the Humanities spirit of many of the new courses and, quite simply, not seen as so exciting an area for research and teaching. It was also around 'meanings' that many courses primarily strove to organise their engagement with media practice and with the vocational desires of many of their students.

b) Language

A convergence point of much new work on media in the 1970s was the posing of questions about 'language'. These were not simply questions of applied linguistics, asking how the media used language, they were questions of a much broader kind about the linguistic ordering of society and consciousness. The structuralist anthropology of Lévi-Strauss, neo-Marxian concepts of ideology, Freudian analysis of the unconscious and, more directly still, the Semiotics of Barthes and Eco, all posed question about language structures or language-like structures. Language was seen as a key, perhaps the key, to the understanding of cultural and social organisation. Semiotics, 'the science of signs', fitted into this intellectual perspective as a practical analytic system which could be immediately brought to bear on the products of the media and a wide range of contemporary cultural expression (as Barthes had playfully demonstrated in his collection *Mythologies*, a text which, again, had an impact in Britain only when the translation became available (in 1972) several years after the original publication of its contents in French). For Media Studies, one of the most exciting aspects of Semiotics was the way in which it allowed application to visual forms – film, television, photography, advertising graphics – thus providing a comprehensive scheme for the study of contemporary meaning-making in a way which traditional strands of linguistics could not. Yet, in actual use, the semiotic project was often less impressive than when outlined as a set of analytic tools.

The basic division between the 'denotations' and the 'connotations' of signs was formally and socially illuminating but in many respects it only served to bring out more clearly the associational character of words and images, a character which previous work in literary and art criticism had for a long time engaged with by using different notions. Semiotics also risked over-rigidity, particularly in respect of the semantic and pragmatic complexity of natural language usage, which linguistics had been trying to cope with from a number of different analytic perspectives.

Even when applied to images, the initial sense of analytic progress could soon give way to problems. Barthes' essay on the photograph (Barthes, 1977) is a case in point, the author having to work rather ingeniously to pin down the ways in which photographs are 'coded' across their twin levels of denotation and connotation, always in a manner very different from that of writing or speech. The difficulty with images was that of finding an analytic unit equivalent to words and a combinatory convention equivalent to the sentence. Without this, the photographic image could seem to be denotatively 'pure' (in comparison, say, with the manifest cultural saturation of a line of descriptive writing) and so 'open' connotatively that analysis, far from achieving scientific precision, was hard put to get beyond the socially impressionistic (the level at which, in fact, Barthes' most successful and provocative essays in cultural criticism are achieved). The search for the 'codes' of a text was frustrated by this problem with the iden-tification and classification of significatory units and with the convincing demonstration of combinatory rules at work. How many 'codes' might be operative in a photograph, where did one 'code' finish and another start? An elaborated language of 'levels' and 'subcodes' produced much of heuristic value but did not consolidate, in substantive analysis, the early theoretical promise of the project. The division between 'paradigm' and 'syntagm' served usefully to denaturalise meaning in a visual text. But specifying the syntagmatic chain (the 'lateral' connections of sign-to-sign) with the precision of conventional theories of verbal syntax was virtually impossible, while listing the paradigmatic (the 'vertical' order of options out of which each present item had been selected) often became unhelpfully open-ended.

These problems were compounded by the extent to which Semiotics was put to the service of ideological analysis, revealing the political and social shapings and purposes of a text in ways not made explicit in the text itself. Such a precise depth analysis, firmly plotting words and images in relation to their ideological origins, was frequently a more hazardous, approximating exercise than Semiotics was usually prepared to admit. Barthes' category of 'myth', a level of signification placed above connotation to give in effect a third, and politically inflected, tier of meaning (see the explication in Barthes, 1972) indicates, at a very early stage in the formulation of Semiotic social critique, the difficulties of doing this kind of analysis. The identification of 'myth' stems not so much from close attention to the levels beneath it as from the analyst's own political sense of what constitutes the 'mythic' in contemporary culture. The procedure is dangerously circular, and whatever results by way of political insight is more a result of the prior political knowledge and intelligence of the writer than of any method or procedure of textual study. Urged on students who had yet to develop such know-ledge or intelligence, the method quickly turned either banal or into an exercise in tortuous self-justification.

The hold of this version of structuralism on media studies was considerably weakened by the shift, beginning in the early 1980s, towards a view of media texts as only being realised into meanings and 'effects' by specific audience interpretations. In some respects, this was a shift from a tightly semantic approach to a more pragmatic one. Only when 'media language' was seen to carry determinate meanings, locatable within the textual structure itself and imposed on audiences with routine success, could the then dominant form of Semiotic inquiry make its claims. When things looked more unstable and contingent, more open to social variation, close scrutiny of texts seemed less reliable a guide, much less a self-sufficient approach.

c) Ethnography

In the mix of approaches and methods which had informed the work of the Birmingham Centre for Contemporary Cultural Studies from the 1960s, ethnographic work (sustained research on behaviours and practices which followed the fieldwork protocols of observation and description developed in anthropology) had figured significantly. 'Anthropology at Home' was the phrase coined by the 1930s Mass

Observation movement to describe their own scrutiny of national cultural and social life, and although the Birmingham researchers had a rather different set of analytic ideas from those of Mass Observation, there was a sense, too, in which much of what they were doing constituted an 'anthropology'. A large part of Hoggart's classic *Uses of Literacy* (1957) was an informal anthropology of a particular period of Northern working-class life, constructed in good measure from the author's own experiences. On the whole, however, the media interests of the Centre had been textually-focused, often intensively and exclusively so. It was the work on different *subcultures* (as for instance, grouped by age, class, musical taste and recreations) which most strongly developed the ethnographic dimension (see, for instance, Willis, 1979). This was reinforced by the emerging feminist emphasis on gendered experience as well as gendered texts.

It was clearly possible to be 'ethnographic' about the media in two main ways: either by conducting detailed inquiries into the producing institutions and their work practices or by focusing on the other end and looking at how readerships and audiences read media meanings into their everyday lives. Although there had been a small number of illuminating sociological studies of the former kind (see particularly Burns, 1977, and also Tunstall, 1971) there were obviously considerable difficulties in getting access to media institutions in the first place and then perhaps (as Burns found out) in getting clearance to publish the results of any investigation conducted within them.

But a new focus on media consumption, on 'audience ethnography', was not primarily a consequence of the difficulties in carrying out production studies. It was a logical following through of the arguments about ideological influence and representational form developed in textual analysis. Such a move was made increasingly necessary by the absence of any audience-related studies on the 'ideological' effect of texts, a lack which was all the more obvious because other approaches to media analysis had often taken a great interest in audiences. On both sides of the Atlantic, the long and varied tradition of 'influence and effects' studies and the more recent and psychologically-informed work on 'uses and gratifications' (departing from many previous models by posing audience *use* of the media as the primary question – see particularly Katz *et al.*, 1974) had produced a vast range of data and arguments. However unsatisfactory and questionable much of this may have seemed from within Cultural Studies, it needed to be directly engaged with not only by theoretical critique but by a body of empirical investigation exposing its limitations and helping to develop new knowledge and alternative ideas.

Stuart Hall, both in his original work and in his explication and critique of major theoretical influences, was the pre-eminent intellectual figure in the Marxist and Semiotic formation of British Media Studies, as well as having a defining impact on the whole Cultural Studies project. His ideas about 'encoding and decoding' (Hall, 1973) had also laid the intellectual framework for direct engagement with audiences by posing the issue of mediation in terms primarily of the transformative practices of production and reception 'codes'. This, although a model strongly influenced by Semiotics, was in some contrast to those approaches which, as I have noted above, concentrated on textual systems with little if any concern for the contingencies either of the production process or of interpretative setting and action. It was a model which drew attention to the interactional character of meaning-making, and thus to the contingency and variability of 'ideological effects' in a manner which challenged any sense of smooth, relentless efficiency.

As many commentators have recognised (and some of the following chapters in this book variously discuss), it was David Morley's 1980 book, *The 'Nationwide' Audience* which was the pioneering project, taking up the Hall model into an empirical research design. Well read in the sociological tradition of audience studies but deriving many of his ideas from the Cultural Studies approach to ideological critique, Morley's study, modest in scale, directly confronted the question of everyday meanings and values and the ways in which television's accounts of world and nation interacted with these meanings in various relationships of domination, negotiation and conflict. The term 'ethnography' was here a suggestive approximation rather than properly descriptive of the method, since Morley's data were gained from discussion with groups of respondents who were mostly from the day or evening classes of various trade and professional groupings attending a local Further Education College. The focus was on the specific nature of interpretation and response to given broadcast texts, screened on video before discussion. This first phase of 'audience ethnography' opened up an important set of questions about interpretative variation and about the limitations of any notion of ideological influence derived exclusively from close textual analysis. It also problematised the simple linking of interpretative position to social class, since Morley found other reception variables which needed to be taken into account, suggesting a more complicated map of audience meaning-making than some had presumed. It is worth noting that Morley's reporting of the conceptual limitations of the 'decoding' model, as these appeared in the course of the fieldwork and in its findings, were often not fully recognised in the work of those who later adopted his basic scheme and attempted to replicate it in other settings.

As the shift to 'ethnography' and the questions it posed become more pronounced (Charlotte Brunsdon (1990) points illuminatingly to the great difference in the number of presented papers on audiences, compared across two meetings of the biannual International Television Studies Conference in the mid-1980s) it started to displace the centrality to the field of text-centred work on influence. However, it did not reduce the interest in text-centred studies of pleasure and cultural value, which were to find new academic encouragement, and more expansive license, within the emerging paradigm of postmodernism. The displacement was reinforced by a further shift, as ethnographic work itself moved away from specific text/viewer interaction towards a broader engagement with the everyday terms and times of viewing, of generic preferences and of the inter-relationship of television use and family life. Morley, a pioneer 'first phase' researcher, whose work related directly to later studies such as those by Ang (1985), Lewis (1985) and Richardson and Corner (1986), was also a pioneer second phase researcher with the publication of his book on *Family Television* (1986). This took the broader view of television–viewer relationships, seeking to explore 'viewing culture' in ways similar to those used by Janice Radway in her celebrated study of the 'reading culture' of a women's lending library (1984).

The broad view quickly became widely replicated in a number of different studies in America, Britain, Europe and Scandinavia. Most of these fell short of the level of ethnographic detail and familiarity with subjects' lives which might be expected in an anthropological study, but they often extended beyond single interview sessions and focus group discussion. However, with the abandoning of the tight agenda around signification which had provided the investigative impetus for 'first phase' studies, the nature of the agenda of inquiry being pursued was not always clear. What the anthropologist Clifford Geertz has called 'thick description', a close rendering of particular behaviours and settings, was sometimes apparent without any clear guiding ideas, explanatory frameworks or critical motives surrounding or informing it. For many of those who had seen media studies as having a radical political character, the lack of critical edge in the new ethnographic work, indeed its tendency towards a certain kind of populism around the activities of 'consumption', was a failing.

The question of 'postmodernism' might be briefly raised here, although towards the end of this chapter I attempt to assess further the general effect on the field of the ideas generated by this confusing term. To the extent that the 'postmodern' condition was seen to involve a radical shift both in the media economy and the general character of cultural goods (for instance, producing new fusions of commodity and style and linking product choices more firmly with purchaser identities) it was aligned with the shift to a more intensive and self-aware consumerism (see Abercrombie, 1990; Lury, 1996). In relation to this, it was argued, 'demand-side' factors (what people were choosing, what they wanted and what they aspired to within proliferating subcultures of consumption) were now in a changed and more influential relationship with the supply-side strategies of product design, marketing and advertising. To some commentators, this was the triumph of late capitalism, or perhaps its gratifying contradiction – to have 'empowered' consumers to the point of overthrowing producer-power, extending choice and increasing quality (a rhetoric, incidentally, widely drawn on in the debate about the deregulation of British television). To others, the dominance of institutions and marketing remained largely unaffected, the 'empowerment' of consumers and the new consumer-focused rhetoric being largely a highly suspect realignment of categories for *experiencing* relationships whose basic power dimension was unchanged.

Certainly, despite having its origins in a search for ideological effects, the swing to audience ethnography seemed ever more closely if ambivalently linked to the first of these perspectives. It engaged with a wholesale movement in culture (and then in theory) which required that far more attention be paid to the dynamics and significance of reception after so much work in the previous decade which had placed viewers and readers, and ordinary viewings and readings, as essentially uninteresting and beside the point as the subjects of inquiry. In this respect, it can be seen to be a useful corrective. But as its sense of theoretical direction wavered, and originality gave way to repetition, its descriptive and implicitly celebratory tones (audiences commended for their transformative, transgressive and resistive energies) became more dominant and defining than critical or investigative development.

d) Summary

These three interconnected aspects of the intellectual formation of Media Studies have a strong cumulative quality, even though the shift to ethnography was a very marked 'turn' in that it had the effect of realigning research priorities and gradually reducing, against initial intentions, the centrality which ideas of ideological reproduction had achieved in theoretical debate, in research projects and also in the teaching syllabus. To pick them out in the way I have done is to exclude many other contributory factors, including counter-currents and alternatives. Yet I believe such a calculated caricature provides a useful route to understanding the conceptual identity of present-day Media Studies and its problems.

Each of the strands which I have identified has developed problems of theoretical coherence and cogency and of substantive analytical development, yet each of them was part of an engagement with issues which still, and rightly, are at the centre of international inquiry and the focus for new thinking. Marxism was a way of addressing the need to connect understanding of the media with economic systems, with political organisation and with structures of power and inequality. Semiotics offered a way of opening up questions about the complexity of textual structures and the various ways in which social meaning was implicated in the conventions of media practice and in the forms of media discourse. The emphasis on audiences and reception was an attempt to register the popular experience of the media by viewers and readers, as knowledge and as pleasure, and to take account of the way in which new patterns of cultural consumption required a rethinking of ideas about the mediation process as an ingredient of everyday living which the perspectives of 'mass communication research' had often neglected. As new fields of inquiry, detaching themselves both from

mainstream Social Science and Literary ways of thinking about the
media, Cultural Studies and then Media Studies became subject to the
sway of theoretical tendencies in a manner which their relatively
modest range of achieved scholarship made unbalancing. But these
ways of attempting to refocus critically on the emerging relations
between media and culture came from a genuine excitement about the
potential of new ideas and a sense of what were real limitations in
existing modes of analysis and evaluation. More detailed accounts of
parts of the story will be found in later chapters.

VOCATIONALISM AND MEDIA STUDIES

I remarked above how the question of vocationalism quite soon
appeared on the agenda of Media Studies, particularly when that
designation was used for an entire degree programme. In the context of
the Thatcher governments of the 1980s, the desire to connect academic
learning with training for new industrial and commercial opportunities
found special favour. The high degree of scepticism shown by the
training bodies and the media industries towards many of the degree
level initiatives could partly be offset by the idea that media production
skills could be exercised by graduates in a range of different jobs and
in a developing sector of small production units (including corporate
and community units) rather than solely in the large, established
organisations. Preparation for journalism was more a problem because
it had clear routes of professional accreditation. In many discussions of
the vocational dimension of Media Studies, journalism and audio-visual
production work were collapsed into a general category of the 'practical' or the 'professional' which made little sense in terms of the
differentiations of the industry itself, even though boundaries here
were becoming more flexible.

Scepticism from employers and professional bodies combined with
the competitiveness of jobs were major sources of difficulty in developing a confident vocational aspect to Media Studies. This difficulty was
sometimes compounded by a lack of clarity about how academically-
grounded studies might ideally relate to a preparation for media careers.
The terms 'theory and practice' proved to be the most unhelpful yet
also the most widely-used of terms in the conduct of debate.

In this simplistic dichotomy, all academic work was classified as 'theory' without regard for the very wide range of intellectual activities comprising study in the area (e.g. history, knowledge of institutions, policy analysis, forms of textual criticism, linguistic inquiry, sociological and psychological studies of influence). 'Practice' was then used to classify all vocational work, even though some of this consisted of abstract ethical protocols, conventions of propriety, ideas about 'quality' and 'standards', etc. To put things in such a way risked marginalising the academic component of courses, since 'theory' could be seen as self-evidently absurd without 'practice' and logically the secondary component when the two were placed in combination (you decided what theory you needed directly and exclusively from what practices you intended to teach). This way of conducting discussion not only blurred important differentiations, even insofar as it referred to what could rightly be called 'theory', it collapsed together 'theories *of* practice' with 'theories *for* practice' and privileged the latter. That is to say, it conceived of theory almost entirely as a set of prescriptions which needed to be taken into practice to be realised. Theories developed *about* practice (about, for instance, the appeal of advertising strategies or the changing use of images in the news or the relations between political and media systems) risked becoming marginal within this view. These could never be *put into practice*, but only in the most anti-scholarly of perspectives could this be taken to indicate a reduced value. Such confusion encouraged poor thinking, including versions of the 'inseparability of theory and practice', a mystical nonsense which clearly had plausibility only on the back of the blurrings and collapses I have previously described.

At the core of the debate was the sound idea that it might be useful if aspirant and trainee media professionals developed a little more by way of a history of the media and a critical understanding of it during their formative studies. But there was never sufficient linkage between degree courses and professional recruitment to make this kind of dialogue and revision of approach actually work. Large numbers of Media Studies graduates were not going into the industry and large numbers of successful recruits to media production and journalism had not done Media Studies.

It is true that some level of practical involvement (in reporting exercises, video projects and script outlines, for instance) was a great aid to analytic understanding and courses which provided work of this kind often substantially increased their real value to students whatever their subsequent careers. However, further development beyond these quasi-academic treatments was not necessary or even, in most cases, desirable. A number of programmes appear to have been encouraged down the highway of vocationalism in ways which many of them may have had opportunity to regret.

One final consequence of 'vocationalism' should perhaps be noted. Of the many commentaries on the growth of Media Studies in the national and educational press, by far the majority are conducted primarily if not exclusively in terms of the field's vocational aspirations and the obstacles to these, as described above. Whilst in the 1970s Communication Studies could be defended or criticised solely in terms of its academic components, it is increasingly the case that Media Studies in the 1990s is discussable only in terms of its career 'promise' and the potential fraudulence of this. As I write, the most recent example comes from an article in *The Times* of 8 October 1997. Its introduction is worth quoting:

> Media Studies is one of the fastest-growing disciplines in higher education. This week nearly 700 eager students are starting a media degree, hopeful that it will secure a job in television or the press. But do too many of them see the course as an easy way in? Do too many leave feeling that they are better qualified than they really are? And do employers prefer to train their staff from scratch? More importantly, are colleges raising false hopes by offering ever more media places when the jobs are not there? (p. 23)

The two accounts which follow, one from inside the media industry, one from a Media Studies lecturer, proceed entirely from within this framework. The 'defence' mounted by the latter reaches its most opti-mistic stage with the comment that newer courses are 'becoming more specialised' in response to the criticism of being 'too wide-ranging' and that prejudice will be broken down only 'if the industry knows what students are learning and if teaching staff have the respect of the industry'.

Here, truly, is the reductive consequence of mishandled vocationalism. A subject area of real intellectual vitality and potential, addressing some of the most engaging issues in contemporary Arts and Social Science debate, is perceived solely in terms of its capacity to achieve a neat 'fit' with industry. This is a one-dimensional version of the area for which many of its leading exponents must share some of the blame and from which it will only recover with difficulty and over the long term if at all. The day following the item, *The Times* carried a story headlined 'Smith gives warning on new media courses' (*The Times*, 9 October 1997, p. 6). This noted how the Culture Secretary, Chris Smith, had 'cast doubt on the quality of the new media and film studies courses being offered by universities'. The primary criteria for this judgement were clear, since his comments came in the context of a Creative Industries Task Force 'set up to discover whether education is failing to prepare students for work . . .' The report noted the perceived poor record of Media Studies in this regard and, seeing work preparation as the area's primary goal, combined a verdict on vocational failings with a questioning of *academic* integrity too ('lacking intellectual challenge and rigour').

In this context, it is not insignificant that Laurie Taylor, the academic-turned-broadcaster whose column in *The Times Higher Education Supplement* has been widely read and enjoyed by academics for two decades, uses a Media Studies Unit as his fictional 'joke' department in the New University of Poppleton. The mix of theoretical pretension and banal populism which seem to constitute much of its syllabus and its staff's research clearly chimes well with general academic perceptions here. It is likely that few, if any, other fields could have given Taylor quite the same possibilities for comic development grounded in consensual prejudice.

TERMS OF REVISION:
MEDIA STUDIES FOR THE NEXT DECADE

Having sketched some of the principal formative ingredients of Media Studies in Britain and assessed its current problems of identity, I want to focus on four themes which I believe will be significant as it adjusts itself to shifts both in the nature of media and of higher education. It follows from the previous section that I regard a radical rethink in respect of vocationalism – both by those who wish to develop down this route and by those who wish to retain for their work a purely academic identity – as absolutely essential and I will not pursue this issue any further here. However, against the negative implications of much of my assessment, I would also like to affirm (as many of the following chapters do in their various ways) the real importance and intellectual vitality of media as an interdisciplinary research focus. This is clear at an international level and it is likely to strengthen rather than decline. What is more difficult to predict is the relationship between this level of research interest, within a developing international research community, and the broader and nationally specific identity of Media Studies as an institutionalised area. A mixed pattern of convergences and separations is likely to continue to develop here. Nevertheless, my four themes link the agenda of research with the agenda of teaching in quite central ways. They are: the engagement with new information technology; a response to the emerging international dimension of media; revision of core theory and methods; and, finally, recognition of changes in surrounding (and partly, constituent) fields.

a) Information Technology

Many programmes of research and teaching now include a range of work on the political, social and cultural consequences of the new IT systems, including the Internet. As more applications and a wider pattern of usage develop, the options for empirical inquiry will increase and the tendency of work in this area towards a speculative agenda will be corrected. IT systems will clearly impact considerably on the nature of broadcast television as well as providing an alternative, screen-based cultural technology for information and leisure. The variously purposive and casual forms of usage of IT, including the potential for extended interpersonal communication at the level of the subcultural or specialist interest group, will pull away from the 'mass' and perhaps even the 'public' emphasis which has been a predominant way of framing media inquiry. The terms of the new 'individualisation' and 'privatisation' will be vital to plot in relation to the more established systems of mediation. A new psychological profile of media use, a response both to the range and the selectability of IT-based options, is likely to emerge and this will have both political and cultural consequences, affecting the distribution and the social relations of information within the society as well as the nature of 'home leisure'. Many researchers in Britain (see, for instance, Silverstone and Hirsch, 1992) have already done valuable work on these questions but they will quickly have to become a broad area of concern in research and in teaching. It will be important that inquiry here keeps in dialogue with the main currents of media research at the level of concepts as well as of debates about substantive shifts and innovations.

b) Response to the 'International'

Framing teaching and research on British media within the context of international developments has become increasingly necessary given shifts in the political economy of media systems. Recently, Downing (1996) has made a strong case for a conceptual review of the whole field, prompted by his studies of transition in Central and Eastern Europe. Of the many obstacles to the adequate representation of the 'international' in Media Studies, the problem of language remains most intractable. Few British students possess the abilities in another language to undertake any kind of meaningful comparative work, so that any other than a superficial sense of the international becomes restricted to broader questions of policy and structure and/or to countries where English is the primary language. This is still of value but falls well short of the desirable. Even under the heading 'European Media Studies', there is a tendency to focus on EU policy and structures rather than the variously diverse or convergent media cultures of constituent countries.

The debate about 'globalisation' has attracted attention and commentary across many Arts and Social Science disciplines, but the freely speculative tones in which it has been conducted (now subject to increasing critique and scepticism) have not aided the development of a grounded sense of the international in media analytic perspectives.

The question of national specificity has also required particular care in British studies, since many aspects of the media system, particularly broadcasting policy, have a uniqueness which is quickly lost to sight in too prompt an attempt at transnational generalisation. Indeed, a significant problem of the literature has been the dominance of models, concepts and criticism from the United States, often applied to British and European instances with minimal modification.

However, there is no doubt that the changing terms of national identity have become a significant factor in media research and teaching in many countries. These cannot be engaged with unless an understanding of a 'native' media system's history and current profile is combined with sustained comparisons and a good sense of the levels at which global structures are emerging.

c) Theory and Method

As this introduction has indicated, and many of the subsequent chapters in this book further illustrate, Media Studies is formed both from an interdisciplinary mix and also from its own distinctive infusion of concepts and critical address. This has shown a tendency towards high theory, critique pitched at the most abstract of levels and often influenced by major figures in recent European social philosophy. Although an empirical tradition has continued, following the line of earlier studies in the sociology of mass communication, there is a need for the eclecticism of the field to become a little less messy and for theoretical work to become more 'accountable' in the sense of being more explicit about its argumentational or evidential bases and therefore about what would count by way of support or refutation. 'Theory' in media studies has often been declaimed rather than argued, and consequently (see Chapter 9) there has often been less a development of theoretical debate than a range of competing and conflicting assertions. Stronger contact between theoretical work and empirical studies would be valuable and might both permit a degree of 'conceptual re-tooling' at middle-range levels (e.g. taxonomies, typologies and analytic classifications) and provide a better setting for methodological development and innovation to take place. There are also a number of areas (Psychology is one, Political Science is another) which are underrepresented within the present mix of the field and, since some of the more recent studies in these areas are convergent with key themes of media research, a revision of the interdisciplinary recipes both for research development and course design would be productive.

Another issue, touched on earlier, is also relevant here. That is the tendency of a significant range of theoretical work in media studies to be offered as critique in a way which can foreclose heavily on the terms of analysis and inquiry. Some 'theories' of this kind are, essentially, evaluations in which analysis and data, if present at all, feature as illustration of the judgement rather than as an argued justification for it or the basis for the building of explanations. The authorial license for 'opinion' enjoyed by literary criticism has been an influential factor in this strand of work. However stimulating and provocative it may be, there is little by way of a real dynamic of inquiry in such writing and the problem I noted above, that of uncertainty as to precisely what arguments or data would serve to question a given proposition, is often chronic.

It is sometimes said in defence of this kind of practice that no academic work can be objective and that to assume otherwise is to work within the terms of an ideology. But conventions of practice in knowledge production can recognise the complexities relating fact to value, along with many other fundamental problems of inquiry, without sliding into such convenient self-confirmatory habits. Sensitive though the issue is, it has to be observed that some of the work on mediations of gender, class and race has too often been more content to elaborate and illustrate general terms of condemnation than to develop further understanding either of the negative processes perceived to be at work or, indeed, any positive alternatives which changed structures and practices might conceivably introduce. It is not surprising that such work has had little impact on public debate or on political policy formulation. A more open acknowledgement of the relation between values, ideas and evidence and of the need for controls, both at the level of general research design and of specific inquiry, would be a welcome prelude to revised practices here.

d) Changes in Academic Context

A number of shifts have occurred in the Arts and Social Sciences since the development of Communication Studies in the early 1970s. Many areas have put questions of 'culture' and 'media' more firmly on their agenda. A greater concern with the complexities of meaning and subjectivity and with the formation of group and individual identity is evident. It is possible to see some of these changes as part of the effect of the 'postmodernism' debate on academic inquiry. This classification has produced vagueness and confusion, but there is little doubt about the modifying impact it has had upon an array of studies, an impact which can be seen as having three dimensions.

Firstly, it has concerned political and social conditions – causing a more intensive discussion of ideas about the nature and direction of modernity as a stage of social and cultural organisation and about its guiding principles. A sense of profound dislocation, an acceleration of change away from continuities and towards qualitatively different kinds of structure, process and experience, has been widely commented upon. As constituents of 'the modern', the media are central to debate about these systemic disjunctions.

Secondly, however, the focus has sometimes been less on 'modernity' than on 'modernism'. The debate has then been one about aesthetics and signification and about the relationship between changing forms and practices of mediation and what is often regarded as the primary cause of these changes – the scale and dynamics of 'consumer culture', the newly commodified and intensively representational terms on which everyday life is lived. Once again, and even more directly, the media and its study become pivotal. The links between a sense of going beyond the condition of modernity and going beyond the aesthetics and the affective order of modernism are often implied but these two distinct planes of 'postmodernism' are routinely subject to confusion or, at least, to an under-definition of their relationship. The issue of how particular shifts in economic and social arrangement relate to changes in expressive form is frequently treated at the level of assumptions, raising major problems with dating and periodisation as well as question-begging on matters of causality. It is worth noting a further problem here. For while arguments about postmodernity as a social state do not easily allow for someone to advocate 'postmodernism' as a *perspective*, arguments about expressive form have allowed and encouraged such a usage, particularly among arts practitioners, where the sense of a self-consciously 'postmodernist' approach can be found. This compounds the more fundamental confusions to which the term is prone.

The third aspect of the general impact has been at the level of theory and methodology. A more reflexive and anxious sense of the limits of knowledge has been introduced into many fields as a result of the postmodernist debate. We can acknowledge this, while recognising that several disciplines have a long tradition of conceptual self-assessment and critique which tends to be ignored by many of those championing the benefits of the postmodern challenge.

The effect of postmodernist debate is, however, not only to be found in the way in which new ideas have been accepted, it is to be found too in the vigorous critique which they have received, a critique which has often mixed reaffirmation with revision. As a result of these combined and various pressures, the terms of social and cultural understanding have shifted and the relations between areas of knowledge have become reconfigured, if less dramatically than is sometimes claimed.

Given the conceptual ferment in many fields surrounding Media Studies, their relatively new openness to matters of culture and identity, how can a distinctive institutional space for the area be maintained? I think this is a very difficult question in 1998. To go for a 'strong' identity means attempting to sustain an academically autonomous project in a way which is undesirable as well as impractical given the field's eclectic profile and its need to keep itself more, not less, alert to what is going on elsewhere. To go for a 'weak' identity, Media Studies as an interdisciplinary site, is intellectually the more honest but risks difficulties with institutional status and has consequences for funding and positioning within national educational policy.

e) Summary

The immediate need for the field in Britain is to regain and defend an academic identity which rejects all 'new discipline' pretensions in favour of programmes involving strong elements of primary discipline training. This latter should be weighted towards Social Science approaches, however much Arts-oriented work features too. It is as a field of culturally and discursively aware social inquiry that study of the media can best be defended and developed in Higher Education. Its engagement with so much of current political, social and cultural change is obvious and could be made firmer. It would also be very much in the interests of many institutions to include a greater amount of other kinds of study opportunity within Media Studies courses, particularly in their early stages but also later too. Sustained work on the literatures and instances of the broader range of Arts and Social Science inquiry is not only desirable for the kind of intellectual development appropriate to degree level study, it is also necessary to make sense of the social and cultural significance of the media themselves. Allowing for a certain arbitrariness in the way in which departments and programmes have come to be named in Britain, a return to the designation Communication Studies to signal a more inclusive and academic setting for teaching about the media might be a great aid in defence and development.

Of course, as I remarked earlier, research into the media has a degree of independence from teaching and the steady international development of media and cultural studies is occurring in ways which pull away from specific national traditions. There are some media researchers, both in the Arts and the Social Sciences, who have retained their teaching base in traditional disciplines and have explicitly distanced themselves from the project of Media Studies, the more so that it has become prone to questions about its vocationalism and its academic integrity. Nevertheless, the majority of researchers are working within contexts defined, at least partly, by related teaching programmes. I have thought it fit in this introductory chapter to give attention to the development of an institutional context because any understanding of the emergence of the field in Britain, of its specific intellectual profile and its present problems of identity and direction, needs to recognise the decisive part played by the rapid growth of courses, and then of departments, within the terms of a more general expansion and revision of national Higher Education.

STRUCTURE OF THE BOOK

In the chapters which follow, discussion frequently touches on, or is shaped by, national particularity, but for the most part it is primarily concerned with issues relevant to the pursuit of media study and research internationally. These are issues to do, for instance, with governing concepts (such as 'mass' and 'code'); with the special difficulties of analysing media texts; with disputes over cultural value; and with the guiding ideas and the disagreements to be found in the new range of work on audiences.

The sequence is primarily thematic, moving from a concern with specific concepts through questions about the analysis of form and then on to questions of interpretation and of cultural judgement. Finally, there is a shift to a more general level of commentary on the intellectual identity of the field and its future, returning to some of the points raised in this introductory chapter. With minor exceptions, each item is being republished using the house-styles for text, notes and references employed in the original. I have used the brief prefatory notes simply to bring out contextual factors which I think might be helpful and to highlight points which seem to me to be of particular significance now, if not always at the time of writing.

REFERENCES

Abercrombie, N. (1990).'The Privilege of the Producer', in R. Keat and N. Abercrombie (eds), *Enterprise Culture*. London: Routledge, 171–85.

Althusser, L. (1971). *Lenin and Philosophy and Other Essays*. London: New Left Books.

Ang, I. (1985). *Watching 'Dallas': Soap Opera and the Melodramatic Imagination*. London: Methuen.

Barthes, R. (1972). *Mythologies* (trans. A. Lavers). London: Fontana.

Barthes, R. (1977).'The Rhetoric of the Image', in *Image-music-text* (trans. S. Heath). London: Fontana, 32–51.

Blumler, J. (1977). 'Communication Studies: Teaching and Research in the United Kingdom', *Communication Studies Bulletin*, 4: 36–40.

Brunsdon, C. (1990).'Quality in Television', *Screen*, 31.1: 77–90.

Burns, T. (1977). *The BBC: Public Institution and Private World*. London: Macmillan.

Downing, J. (1996). *Internationalizing Media Theory*. London: Sage.

Eco, U. (1972). 'Towards a Semiotic Inquiry into the Television Message' (translated from a 1965 Italian original). *Working Papers in Cultural Studies*, 3. Birmingham: University of Birmingham, 102–31.

Hall, S. (1973).'Encoding and Decoding in the Television Discourse', CCCS Stencilled Paper Series, 7. Birmingham: University of Birmingham.

Hoggart, R. (1957). *The Uses of Literacy*. London: Chatto and Windus.

Katz, E., Blumler, J. and Gurevitch, M. (1974).'Utilization of Mass Communications by the Individual', in J. Blumler and E. Katz (eds), *The Uses of Mass Communication*. London: Faber, 19–32.

Leavis, F. R. (1930). *Mass Civilization and Minority Culture*. Cambridge: Minority Press.

Lewis, J. (1985).'Decoding Television News', in P. Drummond and R. Paterson (eds), *Television in Transition*. London: British Film Institute.

Lury, C. (1996). *Consumer Culture*. Cambridge: Polity.

Morley, D. (1980). *The 'Nationwide' Audience*. London: British Film Institute.

Morley, D. (1986). *Family Television*. London: Routledge (Comedia).

Radway, J. (1984). *Reading the Romance: Women, Patriarchy and Popular Literature*. Chapel Hill: University of North Carolina Press.

Richardson, K. and Corner, J. (1986).'Reading Reception: Transparency and

Mediation in Viewers' Accounts of a TV Programme', *Media, Culture and Society*, 8.4: 485–508.

Saussure, F. de (1959). *Course in General Linguistics*. New York: McGraw Hill.

Silverstone, R. and Hirsch, E. (eds) (1992). *Consuming Technologies: Media and Information in Domestic Spaces*. London: Routledge.

Tunstall, J. (1971). *Journalists at Work*. London: Constable.

Willis, P. (1979). *Learning to Labour*. Farnborough: Saxon House.

Chapter 2

'MASS' IN COMMUNICATION RESEARCH

'Mass' has frequently been criticised as a term of description in communications enquiry. In this piece from the late 1970s, I wanted to put forward what seemed to me good reasons for continuing to use the term in describing the major agencies of public communication, while nevertheless recognising that audiences and their experiences could never be characterised as 'mass' without serious distortion.

Multi-channel television and the arrival of the Internet are changing the way we think about the whole process of 'public communication'. It is interesting how much recent work has used and developed Horton and Wohl's idea of the 'para-social' dimension of mediated experience, an idea which I found useful in organising my own arguments here (see, particularly, John Thompson's classifications of interaction in The Media and Modernity, *Cambridge: Polity, 1995).*

At one point in the article, I make what seems now far too strong a case for the way in which mass media systems, through their stylistic strategies of appeal and address, can virtually create the 'social contexts' of their reception by audiences. This, in contrast to most interpersonal communication, which is often sharply sensitive to addressees settings. A recognition of the way in which different social and cultural circumstances of reading or viewing affect what a media item actually means to people would now be necessary, and this would have to modify ideas about media power (see Chapter 7).

Social science has, in the last few years, become a good deal more theoretically anxious and self-critical than it was in the post-war phase of expansion and institutionalisation. This increase in uncertainty has been accompanied by a shift in the focus of research from specific social phenomena to the methods and conceptual vocabulary through which the researcher both 'knows' and systematically explores such phenomena. Although this change in emphasis can be observed throughout the social sciences, it is perhaps studies of communication, given the nature of the concerns, that are especially susceptible to a critical self-consciousness of discourse.

One concept which has been the subject of this questioning attitude has been the concept of 'mass'. At the recent setting up of a British Media Studies Association, for example, a strong objection was raised to the inclusion of the term in the constitution, a number of people being in favour of simply using 'communication' wherever possible. There are a number of problems attending the discussion of this important concept, and these problems do not always seem to have been either adequately articulated or answered. I should like to consider a few of these 'concealed' issues. Dissatisfaction with the term 'mass' has frequently been expressed by cultural historians, sociologists, and social psychologists. Raymond Williams, addressing a London conference called in 1973 to discuss the problems involved in establishing degree courses in communication studies, criticised the notion of 'mass' as being misleading and pernicious (11):

> And so it came about that the study of communications was deeply and almost disastrously deformed by being confidently names as the study of 'mass communication' . . .

Williams related the use of the term back to 'mass society' theory and argued that the disabling characteristics of such a theory were inevitably transferred in applying the adjective to communication:[1]

---

[1] A very recent and useful survey by James Carey of some differences between British and American research traditions in communication gives something of a national dimension to the argument by reporting on the Williams lecture with the comment that 'Americans have never been able to escape, despite their emphasis on small groups, the bias which the word "mass" brings to their studies' (4, p. 411).

The mass metaphor overtook us in its weakest meaning of the large ultimate audience, and then positively prevented the analysis of most specific modern communication situations and of most specific modern communication conventions and forms

The argument that the term 'mass' involves an implicit idea of an undifferentiated, inert aggregate, and thus drastically ignores the varied and specific forms of social interaction is also developed by Robert Escarpit (6), who views the use of the term almost as an 'error' in the social perception of the user:

The concept of mass thus stems from the inability to define or recognize a workable communication organization in a very large group.

An almost identical position is held by Herbert Blumer (2) who asserts that 'there exists little interaction or exchange of experience between members of the mass' and says of the 'proletarian mass' that 'they represent a large population with little organisation or effective communication'.

Let us examine these positions in closer detail. The arguments which Williams brings to bear (11) against the use of the concept 'mass' may be summarised as follows:

1. It unquestioningly inherits the notions concerning large-scale, homogeneous groupings from the mass society theorists.
2. In doing so it also and necessarily assumes that the masses 'are inherently stupid, unstable, easily influenced'.
3. It limits communication studies to 'a few specialised areas like broadcasting and the cinema and what it miscalls popular literature'.

In subsequent publications, Williams has described mass communications as 'a bourgeois concept' (13, p. 136) and, in a detailed commentary on the history of the notion of 'masses' itself, sees 'massification' as a mode of 'disarming or incorporating the working class' (12, p. 163). Escarpit makes a similar point when he argues that the new techniques of diffusion are promoted by the dominant class with the hope that the massification of communication would be an excellent way of reinforcing the existing social structure and of counteracting the spread of class consciousness.

It is not my purpose to deal here with these theories of 'massification' except to make the rather obvious point that a critique of a social process is not the same as a critique of the concept of it. If 'mass communication' is a bourgeois concept, it must be for reasons other than that mass communication systems are, at the moment, largely bourgeois in their strategy – itself a questionable generalisation. I do not believe it either inevitable or even usual for researchers using the term 'mass' to suffer distorted perspectives in the manner Williams describes. In short, I am not convinced that the 'weakest meaning' of the concept has either overtaken us or prevented our attending to variation and complexity. Despite the shared use of the adjective, it does not follow that mass communication is necessarily a concept only 'thinkable' within the social perspective of a mass society theory. Many researchers have employed the term while forwarding arguments grounded in positions ranging from liberal pluralism to the varieties of radical social theory. There is no evidence to suggest that the word exerts some special influence on its users, luring them ever closer to the pronouncements of Ortega y Gassett.

That 'mass communications' has often been defined and researched in questionable ways is of course true, but to make this point is rather different from arguing some inherent flaw in the use of the concept itself. Nor has the notion led inevitably to a belief in the passivity and gullibility of audiences; indeed, the 'uses and gratifications' approach (3) suggests quite the opposite, stressing audience activity while still retaining the word 'mass' in its formulations. Such an example suggests it is simply not the case that, in the words of a British psychologist discussing the issue (1, p. 40).

[T]he bottom is falling out of the 'mass communication' concept as the study of media and their effects begins to take into account the audience's role in the communication process.

Williams' third point, that communication studies have been limited as

ısis being placed on the large-scale networks
ıs equally overstated. Work on the social con-
stics of speech, writing, nonverbal communica-
y has in the last decade gone on, unconstrained
ty, in a variety of contexts, and has influenced
mmunications processes where it has been found
g these specialised modes. There is naturally a vig-
g researchers about the nature and extent of the
case, but the huge increase in, for instance, linguis-
search, bears witness to this influence. So does that
symbolic experience in its analysis of the construc-
tioı. ᴄ ᴜᴜᴜᴜᴜᴜral meaning through the media.

The principal arguments raised by media researchers in opposition
to the notion of 'mass communication' have been, then, (a) a general
objection to what has been conceived of as a discredited social theory
irredeemably linked to elitist anxieties, and (b) a belief that the specific conventions of meaning which make up a given TV programme,
newspaper feature or any media artifact cannot adequately be analysed
unless the very notion of 'mass' is rejected for something more
amenable to specificity and differentiation. Escarpit's formulation of
this latter position is given at the end of his article:

> The result is that the concept of mass is rapidly dissolving to be
> replaced by the puzzling yet far more workable image of an intri-
> cate network of communication channels in which new group-set
> identities are born year after year with corresponding behavioral
> patterns and balance of influences.

It has been my argument that such 'replacement' is unnecessary in
communication studies except insofar as monolithic notions of 'the
masses' – an unacceptable shift from adjective to noun – are seen to be
presumed by the researcher using the term. And there it is redefinition
more than replacement that is required. I want now to discuss those
characteristics of mass communication which, I feel, require us to
retain the contentious concept while yet recognising the important
connections and parallels with other forms of communicative practice.
Many modern researchers have defined and used 'mass communication' in such a way as to make it relatively independent of other 'mass'

concepts. One such account of working definitions is offered by
George Gerbner (8). All of his considered formulations would appear to
escape the censure of both Williams and Escarpit in that they demonstrate a conceptualisation quite conscious of the cruder theories of
'massification' and one able to handle the complex inter-relations at
work in mass communicative practice. According to Gerbner,

> mass communication is the technologically and institutionally
> based mass production and distribution of the most broadly
> shared continuous flow of public messages in industrial societies.

He refers elsewhere to 'mass produced message systems' and a process
which goes 'beyond the limits of face to face and any other personally
mediated interaction'. It is this stressing of the productive and distributive characteristics of the process which usefully forestalls the simple
interpretation of mass communication as 'communicating to *the masses*',
a reifying slip from process to people which, once made, leads to the
problems described above.[2]

The definition offered by Gerbner is one which rightly makes the
adjective 'mass' a description of the *communication system* rather than
the *audience*. Such a usage importantly differentiates 'mass communication' from 'mass culture', a notion which is harder to defend in terms
of a specifiable process.

A similar approach has been adopted by numerous other
researchers, including Phillip Elliott, who concludes his study of
production processes in British television (5) with the remark that '*the
more mass the media* the more inhibitions are placed on a direct
communication process'[3] (my italics). Mass communication is often

---

[2] An early and detailed reassessment of the concept, but one which is, significantly, phrased throughout in terms of 'the mass', is provided by Eliot Freidson (7).
Freidson interestingly concludes that the 'concept of the mass is not accurately
applicable to the audience' but that this 'in no way questions the usefulness of the
concept of the mass for other areas of research'.

[3] In a monograph giving an overview of the field, Denis McQuail suggests a rather
vulnerable compromise when he notes that 'the means of mass communication are
so called partly because they are designed for mass reproduction and partly because
they are appropriate to communicating with a "mass" – an internally undifferentiated
aggregate of people . . .' (10, p. 165).

individually received by people who negotiate its meanings within a complex of social and interpersonal relationships. But to direct attention to this aspect of mass communication – its parasociality (9) – does not require us to change the name of our area of inquiry, and to admit the existence of widely differing readings of the same programme or article does not entail regarding communication through broadcast and publication as just 'another form of human communication'. There are crucial and specific political and social determinants involved in this process, and also a general structure which makes any analysis a rather different matter from the investigation of primary group behaviour, or, for that matter, 'group-set identities', though both these areas may well be relevant to the research.

One of the central characteristics of mass communication is the paradox between its usual individualised mode of reception and its vast productive and distributive networks, as referred to by Gerbner. It is this feature which seems to escape the notice of those commentators who use the example of the crowd, the congregation, and the public meeting in their search for an explanatory historical perspective for the idea of 'mass communication'. For the modern technological means of communication did not simply *extend* the possible size of a communicative network, adding ever more rapid distributive methods, but they also radically altered the *experience* of mass communication, linking it, through the personalised styles of television, radio, and newspaper address, to the registers and repertoires of general social discourse.

There is thus something of a disjunction between the social context of mass communication and the communicative register and style employed, since an informality of address is sustained by a high degree of technical sophistication, professionally assumed roles, and the audience's habitual routines of attention in informal, frequently domestic, settings. The level of integrity of public performance which, say, a 'live' speaker is forced to maintain towards a 'live audience', no matter what rhetorical devices may be permitted, breaks down in modern mass communication as the performance itself is assembled and subsequently attended to at discrete moments in the total communicative process. It is in the gap which thus opens up between these moments that the possibilities arise for social inauthenticity, intentional or otherwise.

The parasocial characteristic is the result both of the depth and range of social knowledge drawn upon variously by audiences to 'realise' meanings from media output, and the variety of styles, formulae, and techniques which are employed by professional communicators to construct and inflect media texts, performances, and therefore to a greater or lesser extent the social meaning experienced (and 'used') by the audience.

Here, the less obviously 'voiced' modes of communication, ones offering to 'reveal' rather than to 'say', are even more important than direct forms of address. One might cite the television mode of drama-tised, realist narrative, now widely used well beyond its conventionally fictive origins, both with and without additional commentary. Through a technologically developed repertoire which constructs an apparently ingenuous discourse, this mode strives to place the audience in the position of chance witnesses to 'social events'. In mass communication the context, a prior social relationship, does not generate an appropriate communicative style; rather, a pre-fabricated communicative style gen-erates and structures a 'context'. One sees Williams' point in stressing the need not to take these socially constitutive styles for granted, but to analyse them in their specific relationships to the primary behaviour they affect to reproduce, and then to relate both to political and cultural formations and practices. The second of these tasks is essential, since mass communication systems often involve a vast number of people receiving simultaneously but independently the communications of a very few, with virtually no facility for contemporaneous effective response. The question is very much one of power, as Escarpit notes.

Since the analysis is concerned with the super-imposition and mutual modification of the varied modes of private and public discourse, achieved within the professional media practices of parasociality, mass communication is not amenable exclusively to functionalist or inter-actionist research. Yet finally the media researcher is primarily concerned with the structuring relationships and processes of mass communication agencies as they contribute to the generation of public meanings, thereby exerting a homogenising influence both on the experiences and the definitions offered. The crucially totalising aspect of this process is well indicated by the word 'mass'.

To conclude, it appears that the discussion of the notion of 'mass' in communication research is still plagued by confusions which relate it directly to the theses of mass society theory, theses which are regarded as being far too culturally alarmist and sociologically unsound to support valid offspring. Other researchers, not directly anxious about general social theory, nevertheless feel that a notion of 'mass communication' cannot do justice to the complex, highly differentiated nature of the phenomenon it labels.

I have tried to show, in response both to Escarpit's claims and to Williams' expressed fears, that a shift in the naming of the area of study is not required in order for theoretical development and argument to progress. A substantial body of communication research exists which is not crippled and crippling in the ways which, it has been suggested, must follow the use of 'mass'; this body of research, moreover, is capable of reflecting critically on its own usages and concepts.

REFERENCES

1. Baggaley, J. 'Communicators in Search of a Language'. *The Media Reporter* 1(2), 1977.
2. Blumer, H. 'The Mass, the Public and Public Opinion'. In B. Berelson and M. Janowitz (Eds) *Reader in Public Opinion and Communication* (second edition). New York: Free Press, 1966, pp. 43–50.
3. Blumler, J. and E. Katz (Eds) *The Uses of Mass Communication*. Beverley Hills, Cal.: Sage, 1974.
4. Carey, J. 'Mass Communication Research and Cultural Studies'. In J. Curran (Ed.) *Mass Communication and Society*. London: Edward Arnold, 1977.
5. Elliott, P. 'Mass Communication – A Contradiction in Terms'. In D. McQuail (Ed.) *Sociology of Mass Communications*. London: Penguin, 1972, pp. 239–258.
6. Escarpit, R. 'The Concept of Mass'. *Journal of Communication* 27(2), Spring 1977, pp. 44–47.
7. Freidson, E. 'Communications Research and the Concept of the Mass'. *American Sociological Review* 18(3), 1953, pp. 313–317.
8. Gerbner, G. 'Mass Media and Human Communication Theory'. In F. E. X. Dance (Ed.) *Human Communication Theory*. New York: Holt, Rinehart and Winston, 1967, pp. 40–57.
9. Horton, D. and R. Wohl. 'Mass Communication and Para-social Interaction'. *Psychiatry* 19, 1956, pp. 215–229.
10. McQuail, D. *Communication*. London: Longman, 1975.
11. Williams, R. 'The Hardening of an Infant's Arteries'. Transcript of lecture given to CNAA Conference on Communication Studies 1973,

in *Times Higher Education Supplement*, London, 7th December 1973. Reprinted as 'Communications as Cultural Science' in *Journal of Communication* 24(3), Summer 1974, pp. 17–25.

12. Williams, R. *Keywords*. London: Fontana, 1976.
13. Williams, R. *Marxism and Literature*. Oxford: Oxford University Press, 1977.

Chapter 3

CODES AND CULTURAL ANALYSIS

———⋙⋘———

Written twenty years ago, this article asks questions about the con-
fusingly various usage of the notion of 'code' in media and cultural
studies. This usage was mainly influenced by structuralist semiotics but,
despite the air of new precision, the term had become very carelessly
applied and was beginning to conceal as much as it revealed about
textual systems and media processes. Stuart Hall's exploratory essays
of the 1970s on media form and culture had the effect of broadening
the application, but Hall nearly always worked with a metaphoric
rather than directly 'technical' idea of codes and he had a strong sense
of the tentative nature of his analyses which was not always to be
found in those who followed his approach. With the shift of attention
to audiences, the idea of 'codes' was, as it were, tipped from text to
interpretation in the idea of 'decoding'. Not surprisingly, given its
limitations in textual study, this notion proved unhelpfully mechanistic
as a way of thinking about the complexity of processes and practices
involved in reception.

The article, however, stays with textual studies and looks at a few
of the problems around 'code' thrown up in the work of Eco, Barthes
and Hall. My position in it is not that semiotics has headed up a blind
alley but that usage of this central term in its vocabulary needs tidying
up both in theory and in application.

In the late 1990s, there has been quite a widespread retreat from
Semiotics. Structuralism has, of course, long declined as an intellectual
fashion, its rigidities and absolutisms criticised beyond redemption.
Yet despite attempts to regenerate a semiotic method from post-
structuralist, sociolinguistic and pragmatic bases, little by way of sus-
tained revival has been achieved and certainly there have been few

45

significant applications to media and cultural research. Klaus Bruhn Jensen's Social Semiotics of Mass Communication *(London: Sage, 1995) is the boldest and most impressive contribution here. A greater awareness of work in descriptive linguistics has perhaps made media researchers more alert to the problems of general analytical schemes whilst the rise of ethnography and the strong sense of contingency encouraged by postmodernist debate have undoubtedly been counter-tendencies.*

Rereading it, I find the piece has moments of density beyond the requirements of the main argument. But the 'code' paradigm was an important and formative phase in the development of the subject area in Britain and much of what is said about it here retains, I hope, its intellectual value.

We mean by code, for instance, a verbal language such as English, Italian or German; visual systems, such as traffic signals, road signals, card games, etc; and so on. (Umberto Eco)

INTRODUCTION

One of the most ambitious projects to be undertaken in the still disputed academic area of 'cultural studies' has been the connecting of the study of linguistic forms with the study of social structure, processes and behaviour.[1] The relationship between society and language or, more broadly, symbolic structures, has long been an important element of social and anthropological research, but the new emphasis is one which seeks to obtain a precision of socio-cultural analysis in keeping both with the 'scientific' levels of systematic investigation achieved by modern linguistics and, quite often, the 'scientific' ambitions of much radical social theory. The system of a particular language and the

---

[1] Many examples could be given of the centrality of the approach but perhaps Hall (1973) is most illustrative: 'My purpose is to suggest that, in the analysis of culture, the inter-connection between societal structures and processes and formal or symbolic structures is absolutely pivotal.'

system of the particular society which uses it are seen to be in an important, mutually determining relationship – such that linguistic study of a certain kind offers inroads into an understanding of a society and its characteristic processes. Linguistic paradigms have also been used in the study of a whole range of cultural phenomena, including those not previously thought of as having directly linguistic dimensions, such as photography, dress and aspects of social behaviour and organisation. A widened meaning of 'language' has emerged.

Many of the researchers who have addressed themselves to this broadly sociolinguistic enterprise (as well as work in sociolinguistics from a social science base there has been a range of structuralist, semiotic and literary critical influences) have had to resort at some point or other to the notion of 'code', which they have used with varying degrees of emphasis and according to a number of definitions. In this article I propose to examine some of the problems of these usages, concentrating on dominant tendencies within the area of cultural studies/communication studies.

CODES

Although 'code' is widely used in general speech and writing to indicate levels of rule-system ranging from the closure of Morse code (a tight set of correlations) to the relative openness and generality of a code of norms or of conduct (which might at times be describable as the unspoken and implicitly organised tendencies of behavioural propriety) in the area of linguistic social research something close to the idea of a set of rule-governed operations is usually indicated by the term. That is to say, the usage points towards something closer to Morse code than to the normal uses of code of manners, where an altogether more loosely-arranged set of guiding conventions, a lower level of determinations, is suggested.

It is worth noting here that as well as different levels of *systemic organisation* being involved, there is also a matter of *transformation* to be considered. Morse code allows one, by precise equivalents, to transmit language in the form of a broken audio tone or light beam; a code of manners, whilst it certainly exerts some systematic pressure on behavioural choice, does not strictly speaking *encode* anything at all. It may give a socially determined coherence and a regulated means of expression to areas of social experience but expression is not synonymous with *transformation across systems*. On this count, many contemporary uses of code in cultural analysis appear to be closer to code of manners than to morse-code, though there is frequently assumed to be a high level of systemic inter-connection at work, as I shall discuss later.

A number of introductory texts in the area slide around this issue rather confidently, as if code suggested a spectrum of relatively unproblematic systemic states and that the shift from semaphore to social behaviour was purely one of degree. It is true that matters of degree enter into the question of how the production of human and social meanings is variously organised and controlled but that is not to say that they are 'mere' matters of degree or that they do not require careful differentiation. In fact, most confusions in cultural code theory seem to be due less to the researchers artfully abusing the term as to their falling victims to its general imprecision when on its own and its wide range of meanings in specialised contexts.

The concept 'code' has entered communications and cultural studies in Britain through three rather distinct lines of research:

1. The technological paradigms of much early work on 'communication theory', paradigms in which the terms 'encoding' and 'decoding' are borrowed from information theory and telecommunications and indicate the conversion of 'message' into 'signal' and the reverse (Shannon and Weaver, 1949). This usage is still operative in many models and perspectives seeking a unified (and therefore often highly abstract) general theory of communication. Combined with genetic and psychological perspectives, it is present also in the influential work of Bateson (1951) and Wilden (1972).

2. The class-specific, sociolinguist theories of Basil Bernstein and his fellow researchers, notably those at the University of London Institute of Education. Here code is defined as 'frame of consistency' and 'social structuring of meanings' (Bernstein, 1971). In a development of the concept (Hasan, 1973), codes are seen to be related to the 'semantic structure of a message' both as this is determined by 'social relationships' and as it, in turn, determines those 'varieties of language' which are in fact the 'verbal realisations' of the codes, here described primarily as 'codes of behaviour'.

The categories 'restricted' and 'elaborated' are, of course, the code forms most often referred to in this research tradition. Widely influential in education, the theory has been used elsewhere, including political sociology.

3. The developing project of semiotics as a general approach to the study of social meaning linked to a structuralist cultural analysis. In this perspective, the location of individual meaning elements within rule-governed wholes – signifying systems – is a fundamental proposition, quite often extended to all social meaning. The particular level of closure indicated by the use of the term code is frequently clear if implicit in the various and detailed theoretical and analytic treatments, treatments which usually involve the identification of separate codes at work in a given text or piece of social action. Here, Barthes (1971, 1972), Eco (1972, 1976), Burgelin (1972) and Hall (1973) have been key influential texts, whilst Lévi-Strauss (1963) provided, quite early on, a structuralist, anthropological version of socio-textual analysis. (See also Geertz, 1973 and Leach, 1976.)

Although research in communication studies has produced what appears at times to be a conflation of these three broad uses of 'code', any points of convergence must be considered in the light of the rather different implications, both in terms of the notion 'systemic organisation' and that of 'transformation', which the approaches carry. We must also note the location of these approaches within differing social or political theories. Furthermore, although 'code' is most often used as a 'language–society' bridging concept, usage varies in the emphasis placed on social or linguistic characteristics – to the extent, that in some cases, the notion hardly seems to be 'bridging' at all but to be conceptualised as lying almost entirely within the distinctive territories of either the linguistician (language form, dialect, register) or the sociologist (socialisation, belief-system, social structure). Nevertheless, perspectives 2 and 3 above can be related (and both distinguished from perspective 1) insofar as they both address themselves, if at times only implicitly, to one of the central issues in modern 'cultural studies' and, indeed, a central one in much political and social research – ideology, variously and problematically related to consciousness and language. Here, the relation of 3 above to media analysis is my prime concern.

It is the development of research in this area, stemming from a resurgence in Marxist work on social knowledge, which has helped to promote the use of linguistic paradigms in social research (in combination with other influences like the 'new' anthropology), although the emphasis on textual analysis and the 'reading' of ideological formulations has not gone unchallenged in Marxist media research.[2]

Bernstein's concern with 'the structures of cultural transmission' thus connects with Umberto Eco's more formalistically ambitious belief that 'Semiology shows us the universe of ideologies arranged in codes and sub-codes within the universe of signs' (Eco, 1972).

It has been claimed that, at one level, 'an ideology may be defined as a system of semantic rules to generate messages' (Eliseo Veron quoted in Camargo, 1974) so that the appropriateness of the concept code to ideological analysis is apparent. It offers the possibility of plotting 'cultural transmission' and its constitutive language-systems with a gratifying sense of precision. Though less important, it also seems to be the case that its connotation of covert dealings has won for the term an extra, if improper, allure in the eyes of some critical researchers investigating political and social knowledge as perpetrated 'myth'.

One final point I would make by way of preliminary observation is that the theoretical and definitional problem of the 'tightness' of internal correlations within a specific 'code' and also the problem of the precise character of the transformations (if any) being worked are often compounded by the notion of a plurality of codes or code systems at work in the same text, artefact or communicative behaviour. That is to say, the relationship of these systems, codes and subcodes (see Eco above) to one another – as alternative or jointly contributory factors in the production of social meaning (and the latter in ways involving varying degrees of overlap, superimposition or what Barthes calls 'imbrication' – further troubles the theory of codes in cultural analysis.

---

[2] Murdock and Golding (1977) are quite emphatic in opposing what they see as a dangerous bias towards 'readings' of media artifacts and their ideological structures which are insufficiently grounded in social and economic analysis. Semiotics and socio-literary approaches (including work in cultural studies) come in for particular criticism.

CODE AND MEDIA TEXTS

'The 'unity' of current affairs television' (Hall, 1976) illustrates some of the difficulties in using 'code' in an analysis of media texts and professional media practices. In a theoretical foreword to the case-study of an edition of *Panorama* which forms the centrepiece of the paper, it is argued that:

> Several different codes are required to construct the meaning of a message; it is the product of several meaning systems in combination.

Initially, these different 'meaning systems' appear to be identified as the sound and visual tracks of a television programme, tracks which operate both independently (horizontally) and in combination (vertically). Later in the piece, however, code is used in a broader, richer sense:

> Connotational and ideological codes are therefore at work, organising the elements of the message, as well as those codes which enable the broadcaster, literally to 'get a meaning across'.

The distinction indicated here, between denotational and connotational coding, suggests important differences within the range of relationships possible between codes and a primary language system, differences to which I shall return later.

Even further into the main *Panorama* study, which is concerned with, among other things, the strategic, rhetorical control over 'discussion' exerted by James Callaghan in a 1974 Election Special, code appears to signal a still more general and yet apparently more categorisable and discrete system of meaning. Referring to Callaghan's undermining of some previous comments made by William Whitelaw, the authors note:

> Callaghan accomplishes this by explicitly signalling, and then openly playing with, the fact that two codes are at work – the political code (hard opposition and attack) and the 'Parliamentary Debate' code (rudeness is a sort of polite game).

Callaghan is later said to block the intervention of the studio chairman by resorting to a gambit invoking the idea of the responsibilities of the politician – a ploy which the researchers see as an appeal 'in the name of a "higher duty" – (a more powerful code)'.

It is clear, I think, from these examples alone that the linguistic levels, the degrees of systematicity and the kinds of organising influence of the 'codes' variously indicated in the paper are difficult to subsume within a single, unifying concept of codification. From the extract above, it is hard to judge the status of the parenthesised glosses – are they elements of, or summaries of, the respective codes? If the latter, just how useful is it to call 'hard opposition and attack' the 'political code'? If the former, what are the codic relationships involved and on what specific political set of generating principles do they systematically depend? Although initially the term seems to promise the mapping of highly structured and socially determined systems of linguistic behaviour it quite soon becomes used to denote the inflection of any utterance in the televised discussion towards this or that rhetorical strategy and to denote, too, the principles and policies which the strategies are used to articulate and uphold (the 'code' of the broadcaster consisting presumably of arguments adducing professional broadcasting values, the 'codes' of the politician being variously grounded in notions of public responsibility and representative authority as these are interpreted through party perspectives).

This inadequately theorised shift away from natural language equivalents ('getting meaning across') towards the social inflections and implications of specific utterances (where the notions of register and rhetoric would seem equally useful *given the levels of system evidenced*) is a slide observable in a number of cultural studies' analyses making central use of 'code'. The employment of the term to describe almost any discernible cultural convention or behavioural pattern, whether notions of transformation or of a discernible systemic invariance are appropriate or not offers an obstacle to clarity of analysis and I shall return to this aspect of the problem later.

In the case of 'The "unity" of current affairs television', even if one allows the argument that there is a plurality of very different *kinds* of code at work at varying levels in the total discourse of the programme analysed, there is considerable difficulty in relating these codes to each other within a notion of the total discourse's *determination*. In the latter part of the analysis of the *Panorama* programme Callaghan is seen to 'break the rules' by taking over a chairmanship role, thus securing a sizeable 'win' in terms of the televised contest of arguments. Nevertheless, the authors of the paper go on to remark that 'we think it can be established that, within the rules and codes of the programme, a "Callaghan win" is the reading which this programme prefers.' The notion of the 'preferring' of one reading of a text rather than others by mechanisms *within the text* which weight possible interpretations in one direction is central to much of the research at the Birmingham Centre. It has led to subtle studies of the reading act as one involving the realisation of meanings through the complex negotiation of differing interpretative frames with textual devices, some of which tend to close-off the apparent choice of interpretation in a number of ingeniously ingenuous ways – for instance, the variety of naturalistic techniques used in film and television programme construction. Such textual 'work' is identified by the cultural studies researcher and used as a sort of constellation of clues which permits a tracing-back to, and reconstruction of, the ideological formations ('fields of force' of meaning and value) within which the text was produced.

Yet to return to the *Panorama* example, it is unclear how this process of 'preferring', if it is to be theorised as a function of the 'codes of the programme', relates to those other codes mentioned earlier by the researchers – the codes contributing to the *transmission* of visual and verbal meanings; those involved in 'getting the meaning across'. What we apparently have is a situation in which Callaghan breaks a code only to have that breach registered as a 'win' within the 'codes of the programme' and transmitted as such through what were earlier called 'the several different codes required to construct the meaning of a message'. It is not made clear how these 'metacodes' of the programme somehow negate the codes at work in the debate which forms the programme's subject or how the various verbal and kinetic codes combine with the visual codes of television discourse to augment or lessen the 'dominance' achieved at other levels. One has the impression that code is being used quite frequently in lieu of 'inflection', 'register' or even 'principle' and is therefore giving to the analysis a far tighter sense of traced and inter-connected configurations of determined meaning than is actually evidenced. At the point in the paper where the authors develop their notion of 'preferred reading' they remark:

However, *it is in the nature of all linguistic systems which employ codes*, that more than one reading can potentially be produced: that more than one message-structure can be constructed (my italics).

It would be useful to know, here, just what sort of linguistic systems do *not* employ codes and through that knowledge to find out what the conditions of employment are as understood by the researchers.

Codes and Determinations

In an earlier, influential article on 'The determinations of newsphotographs', Hall (1972*b*) follows Barthes and Eco by setting out to show how various levels of coding operate to constitute the meaning (in its structured complexity) of a specific photograph. He theorises the notion of code level used in the 'Unity' paper with the comment:

> Thus, whereas the codes which 'cover' the signifying function of the linguistic sign at the denotative level are relatively closed 'sets', from which quite tightly constructed rules of transformation can be generated: codes of connotation, constructed over and above the denoted sign, are necessarily cultural, conventionalised, historical.

Hall, again following Barthes (1972) refers to the latter area as one of 'second-order' meanings. A few pages later, he notes in a partial re-working of the same point, that:

> . . . denotative codes are relatively 'closed', connotative codes are relatively 'open'. Connotative codes are tight enough to generate meanings of their own, but these codes do not produce one invariant meaning – they tend to delimit meanings *within a preferred range or horizon*.

However, in a rather confusing way, Hall then goes on to see the preferred *range* of the connotational level, which he calls 'this polysemy', as the field *within which* a further preferring operation (operated by codes of preferencing within the text?) secures a narrower 'dominant reading among the variants' – a closure of the (apparent) openness or polysemy.

To what extent these further codes operate with an invariance of internal relationships Hall does not say, nor does he question the suitability of the term 'coding' to describe the variety of levels of meaning-producing activity which his paper details. He focuses on the question of what happens when a reader/viewer does not take the 'preferred reading' but either produces some modified version of this through 'negotiation' or else 'takes' a radically different meaning from that 'preferred'. The question is dealt with by Hall in terms of his theory of 'coding' and exposes, I think, some further problems in that theory.

The primary issue which Hall wants to address is that of differenti-ated readings of the same text; the way in which different meanings are constructed on the same 'site' and from the same textual system exerting its 'cueing' pressures. If the argument is that 'it is in the nature of all linguistic systems which employ a code, that more than one reading can potentially be produced' then Hall is intent here on giving that position a detailed theoretical grounding. To do this, he refers to a paper by Eco (1972) in which a typology of codification is developed in the context of a semiological argument and a detailed definition is offered of the concept 'code'.

> By code we mean a system of communicative conventions paradig-matically coupling term to term, a series of sign vehicles to a series of semantic units (or 'meanings') and establishing the structural organisation of both systems, each of them being governed by combinatorial rules, establishing the way in which the elements (sign-vehicles and semantic units) are syntagmatically concate-nated.

After giving a number of examples of different sorts of code Eco suggests, importantly it seems to me, that:

> After these definitions let us restrict the concept of code to the basic conventional systems, it is in fact with these elements that it is possible to then work out 'secondary codes'; or 'sub codes' more or less systematized, which furnish new lexical elements or give a

different connotation to lexical elements contained in the basic code.

So it is argued that the 'more or less systematised' clusterings do not qualify for the term 'code '– a notion which is reserved for the 'basic conventional systems' from which the 'subcodes' operate as a sort of fine-tuning of meaning, related to social contexts and specific areas of discourse (Eco discusses, among other subcodes, the aesthetic sub-code, the erotic subcode and the montage subcode). Nevertheless, Eco is still tempted to use 'code' in ways which seem to conflict with his earlier definition, suggesting at one point that 'the conventions at the basis of gastronomic choices . . . form a code' without specifying just how these satisfy the definitional criteria previously argued for. Moreover, it is clear that his offered distinction is not directly parallel to connotation/denotation nor to Hall's comments on 'second-order' (and, by implication) 'first-order' meaning.

In the course of his initial discussion, Eco also refers to what he terms 'aberrant decoding'. The example he offers of this process rather exotically involves the manner in which the Achean conquerors of Crete would interpret the stucco relief in the Palace of Knossos. The iconography of these paintings, their use of certain conventional corre-lations in artistic representation (e.g. stick – sceptre, brown face – youth) constituted a code which was culturally specific to the artist's community and therefore one which, it is argued, was not available as part of cultural experience to the new, invading culture. Insofar as the invaders understood or 'made sense' of the paintings, Eco continues, they did so in an *aberrant* way – one not in alignment with the moment of encoding.

It is this idea which Hall develops in his discussion of the 'preferred reading' of newsphotographs (although he is anxious to remove the pejorative idea of 'aberrance' from what he wants to see as the pro-gressive possibilities of the differential reading – an approach actually advocated by Eco himself in a *post scriptum* comment to the English translation of his paper). Hall re-works the idea of 'aberrant decoding' in terms of political and class-related behaviour in contemporary society; in terms of a theory of ideological reproduction. Using a ter-minology taken from Frank Parkin's work on social meaning systems (Parkin, 1971), work which suggests how it is that differing versions of

the same behaviour or communication can be 'read' as a result of differing interpretative frames generated by differing socio-economic
locations, Hall suggests that:

> It is possible for the reader to decode the message of the photo
> in a wholly contrary way, either because he does not know the
> sender's code or because he recognises the code in use but *chooses*
> *to employ a different code* (italics in original).

In Eco's illustration there was a disjunction of geographical culture
(and to some extent of historical time) between the encoding conventions and whatever interpretative frames interested Acheans chose to
use on the Knossos reliefs. Moreover, the convention system itself was
squarely founded upon one-for-one correlations – at its lowest level
therefore (for there were presumably more nuanced levels of expressive convention) it was tightly systemic. One wonders how the modern
'oppositional' (aberrant) reader/decoder of a newsphotograph manages
to achieve anything like the codic ignorance of someone from 'another
culture' or the related degree of codic independence when he or she
'chooses to employ a different code'. In fact, this second case, the
willed employment of a code *known to be different* from the one 'preferred', seems to be more a case of 'double decoding' than anything close
to Eco's idea of aberrance, since a conscious, cognitive shift follows the
recognition, by the reader, of 'preferred codes' at work and this shift
involves a meta-level of interpretation – an active, aware reading
against the rhetorical grain of the text as that grain is 'realised' at the
lower level of reading. There are problems, in both cases, concerning
the nature of meaning production/transmission and the levels of
consciouness involved – and these problems are rather blurred over by
the manner in which 'code' is used.

If, to use Hall's illustration, a newspaper reader chooses to interpret
the photograph (of a policeman being kicked in the face by an anti-
Vietnam-war demonstrator) within an interpretative framing developed
from the belief, say, that 'the cause of anti-Vietnam war demonstrators
is a just and legitimate one in our society; the forces of law and order
are performing here a repressive political function', how does this
interpretation get made? How does the general attitude (a political
code?) determine or combine with the lower-level interpretative

procedures by which such things as facial expressions, aggressive postures, the 'civic' resonances of the confrontation (regardless of the particular attitudinal versions of these) get 'read off'? What is critical here is the degree of variation and independence of specific interpretative processes, their reliance on common cultural ground at certain levels of operation, including much denotative work, and their differences – as interpretative procedures – at 'higher' levels of cultural connotation. One should not exclude the possibility that middle-range variations may in some cases be subsumed within the same higher level interpretative frame (thus, for instance, a general deploring of violence against the agency of civil 'law and order' could be mediated through a variety of different positions on, say, the role of the police in public demonstrations, the legitimacy of such demonstrations and the legitimacy of the United States's operations in Vietnam).

Hall's complex typology, a treatment of the successive levels of signification at which a cultural text is 'worked' or 'inscribed', perhaps commits him to an ambitiously wide range of reference for the idea of 'coding'. It refers at one level to the photograph as iconic sign, one employing 'formal-denotative codes' and moves through a number of levels of more or less technical/professional 'work' (news production, retouching, cropping, page composition etc.) until it makes contact with the culturally expressive meaning-systems at the 'ideological level' – the level at which Parkin's typology is taken up to aid the mapping of differentially realised ('taken') meaning.

This layering of the analysis upwards to the ideological level does not mean that culturally informed decisions are not taking place at the more fundamental levels of 'working the sign' however, as Hall reminds us. Nevertheless, the overall structuration which Hall suggests by his notion of determining 'codes' is not brought out in the analysis with the degree of systemic inter-relatedness which the theoretical preface to his article promises.

THE PHOTOGRAPH: CODE (OR ANALOGUE? OR ANALOGIC CODE?)

I have traced Hall's use of code in cultural analysis, both as a theory and as an analytic tool in specific research, in relation to the work of Eco. In choosing to discuss work on the photograph I hope to have provided a context in which the consideration of 'codes' can be pushed one stage further back to primary concepts, since the question of whether the photograph is a 'coded' form at all has been examined, with differing conclusions, both by Roland Barthes, perhaps the most influential of the continental semioticians, and, in a critical commentary on Barthes, by Hall.

One of the difficulties of talking about a 'visual language' in respect of photography is the lack of anything equivalent to the denotative vocabulary and regularised syntax of natural language. Before discussing the arguments of Barthes and Hall in this respect, it might be useful to offer an example of the sort of problems that can arise as a result of this difficulty. Such an example is afforded by Camargo (1974) in which there is developed an 'ideological analysis' of a *Daily Telegraph* magazine cover. The cover shows an expensively but conservatively dressed man and woman standing some distance apart with two identically dressed children, a child on the right-hand side of each adult. Moreover, symmetry is further emphasised in that each adult holds a child by the left hand. At the left 'heel' of the man sits a dog. Behind them is a terraced pathway and behind that, dominating the upper half of the frame, is a castle. Having earlier told us, as a general point, that 'denotative meanings are given by the code whilst the connotative meanings are given by subcodes' (here, following Eco) Camargo argues that 'The denotative meaning of this picture is: the couple, their children and their castle (home).' As many of my students have pointed out, there is some difficulty in finding 'denotative' evidence of the possessive ('their children', 'their home') in the photograph. Anyway, what would such evidence look like? What seems to have happened is that Camargo has 'read off' possession at the 'connotative level' (and I would certainly not wish to argue against this particular visual registering of the culturally obvious) and then incorporated (rendered back) these significations into her theorisation of the denotative. The use of denotative/connotative differentiation in the cultural analysis of visual texts needs perhaps to retain some flexibility and sense of dialectical relation if it is to avoid problems such as this; problems which frequently follow from too rigid an attempt at applying a natural language model. This returns us to some of the more provocative theoretical considerations on photography of Barthes.

In a widely-cited though quite often misunderstood paper, 'Rhetoric of the image' (1971), Barthes refers to the 'absolutely analogic' nature of the photographic component of an advertisement for *Panzani* pasta. What he has to say about this has a general relation to much of my earlier discussion of codification:

> The photograph implies, without doubt, a certain arrangement of the scene (framing, reduction, flattening) but this event is not a *transformation* (as a coding might be). The equivalence appropriate to a true system of signs is lost and a quasi-identity is posed. In other words, the sign of this message is no longer drawn into an established reserve i.e. it is not coded, and we are dealing with the paradox (to which we will return) of a *message without code*.

Barthes' use of the ideas of rule-governed transformation and an 'established reserve' is here deployed against the notion of the coded photograph, although clearly he is aware of a certain level of intervention, of a 'worked' discontinuity between, in his terms, signifier and signified. Nevertheless, for him the photograph is 'analogic' since its relationship to what it represents is one of direct resemblance in contrast to the arbitrary ('digital') codings of, say, natural language.

Since Barthes' position has produced much comment it is worth quoting a later passage in the same paper where he develops the argument:

> In the photo – at least at the level of the literal message, the relationship of signifieds to signifiers is not one of 'transformation' but of 'recording', and the absence of a code clearly reinforces the myth of the 'natural' photograph; the scene is there, captured mechanically, but not humanly (the mechanical is here the guarantee of objectivity). Man's intervention in the photograph (framing, distance, lighting, focus, filter etc.) all belong in effect to the plane of connotation; everything happens as if there was at the beginning (even Utopian) a brute photo (frontal and clear) on which man disposed, thanks to certain techniques, signs drawn from a cultural code.

So Barthes here distinguishes between cultural codes and the special case of the photograph's denotative method, which he earlier contrasts with the culturally constituted, transformative activity of drawing.

It is understandable that the passage has raised a few problems. The less than satisfactory remark, given the main thesis concerning 'objectivity', about the absence of the codes 'reinforcing the *myth*' of photographic naturalism (is Barthes arguing here that such naturalism is an illusion?) and the shift to flourishingly dramatic hyperbole at the end are characteristic of a style which frequently cultivates enigma at just those moments when the diligent reader is seeking to follow the argument between the insights. There is also the question – it may be one of translation – of the relationship of 'analogue' to 'analogic code', since Barthes talks of the latter at one stage in his paper and it would be difficult to argue that the photograph's 'message without a code' was, in fact, the product of an 'analogic code' without being perversely unhelpful even by the standards of Barthesian playfulness.

Just how 'natural' Barthes thinks photographic denotation to be, allowing for his decidedly whimsical phrasings, has worried some commentators on his paper. Trevor Millum, in an introduction to the Birmingham Centre translation of the piece, remarks:

> surely the pictorial message is coded in the photograph no less than in the sketch? Does not the camera *itself* carry out the coding? Otherwise why is it that children, and members of cultures unfamiliar with photography, have to *learn* to interpret photos?

Millum goes on to comment that a refusal of the notion of the uncoded photograph allows 'the photo (to) be replaced within the mainstream of semiological thought'. However, he hardly engages with the argument (nor perhaps has space to do so) in the detail needed to refute Barthes' claims. The suggestion that the 'camera itself' carries out the coding is not sufficiently clear as a proposition to do more than its immediate function of rhetorical questioning – in fact, if anything it tends to suggest that 'mechanical' level of operations referred to by Barthes himself. Similarly, though the point about 'learning to interpret' photographs is clearly relevant, the central factors to be borne in mind here are, I imagine, precisely 'reduction', 'flattening' and 'framing' together with other, related qualities – characteristics which Barthes allows as interventionary moments in the production of the 'resemblance' but which he disallows as grounds for talking of 'codification'. Moreover Barthes himself, in the course of his paper, draws our attention to the child's learning to 'read' that something is a picture.

Stuart Hall, in an essay on documentary journalism, 'The social eye of *Picture Post*' (1972*a*), takes issue at greater length with Barthes' line of argument (as well as Barthes, he cites Metz, Pasolini and Bazin as being at least half-supporters of indexical theories). Like Millum, Hall stresses the importance of regarding the photograph as a product of codes, if unique and complex ones. Hall is concerned specifically with the components of the 'rhetoric of visual exposition' employed by the *Picture Post*, noting particularly layout, captioning and characteristic content. He contrasts the modern colour supplement (photographic romanticism) with the *Post*'s use of 'realist' black and white and notes that we are not dealing 'with "natural" versus "conventional" photography but with *two different codes*' (italics in original). Yet apart from these remarks on the socially constructed connotations of photographic tones, Hall, again rather like Millum, does not actually introduce any more social factors into a theory of photographic production than did Barthes in the paper under criticism.

At times, it seems as if Barthes' mistake is seen to be that of placing the analysis of photography at least partially into some enclave of 'innocent denotation'. Phrases in Barthes' arguments like 'guarantee of objectivity' serve to cause anxiety in this respect, although such usages are nearly always specific and qualified, as well as often having more than a touch of stylish irony about them. Overall, it is hard to see Barthes' approach as one promoting a theory of pre-cultural signification; for Barthes the photograph is a thoroughly cultural form though he wishes to retain a recognition of its distinctive method of sign production. Although imperfectly argued, his comments still constitute a necessary object of address for those researchers who wish to develop a visual semiotics.

Throughout my discussion I have illustrated a central premise at work in the use of 'code' in cultural analysis – that cultural conventions and their variants operate with a degree of internal coherence and regularity comparable to that found in natural language. This premise, which is a very important structuralist thesis, usefully de-naturalises the operation of meaning-systems in society and allows an emphasis (though one not often developed in detail) on their historical and social origins and their rôle in constituting the configurations of social reality. In doing so, however, it often fails to monitor the implications of the linguistic paradigm at each level of application and in terms of each specific piece of analysis. When Hall, in 'Determinations', remarks that 'in language, there is no message without a code' two questions are prompted – what is to count as 'language' and is the 'code' here synonymous with language or is it a secondary system acting upon it? It is worth noting, too, that the above quotation seems out of alignment with that reference made in the later 'Unity' piece to 'linguistic systems which employ codes' as if to suggest that some such systems did *not* employ them.

Many studies informed by semiotics consider natural language to be, as it were, the 'primary code', though the extent to which it is its levels of systemic determinacy or its 'transformative' work within perception and experience (experience as a codification of reality) that gain it this title is often unclear. Hawkes (1977) summarises the underlying postulates of much work in social semiotics thus:

> In short, a culture comes to terms with nature by means of 'encoding', through language. And it requires only a slight extension of this view to produce the implication that perhaps the entire field of social behaviour which constitutes the culture might in fact also represent an act of 'encoding' on the model of language. In fact, it might itself be a language.

This is perhaps a more qualified position on the issue of 'society as discourse' than many researchers in the field would adopt – the shift from 'on the model of' to 'itself be' is crucial and is not always signalled quite so clearly.

CONCLUSIONS

I have suggested throughout this paper that many researchers have been unclear in their use of the term 'code' in studies of human communication and that, whether deriving from a positivistic technological model or from the hypotheses of semiology (sometimes less hypotheses than presumptions), the term often seems to offer more than is actually rendered in the aiding of our understanding of human signification and of the social construction of meaning. Paramount here is its taking-for-granted, without adequate research, of high levels of systemic organisation among cultural phenomena, levels often involving a fixity of relationships. This is theorised in forms often derived from structuralist linguistics and leads too often to a rigidity of analysis similar to many functionalist explanations in social science; systems being inferred from 'typical' transformations and correlates which in fact only constitute a very small number of actually observed and plotted relationships.

A further problem is that of the relations within and between cultural codes and subcodes, since in many cases the choice of system-title used in a piece of research (the journalistic code, the code of the programme, the erotic subcode etc.) seems quite arbitrary and does not facilitate either referral downwards to primary signification nor upwards into a theory of ideological reproduction (how the 'structures' are put 'in dominance').

The precise *nature* of the inter-relationships proposed between different levels of signifying practice is often only minimally suggested, even where some notion of 'levels' informs a classificatory system. The problem of codetermining and conflicting codes frequently remains unaddressed.

A recent piece of published research (Brunsdon and Morley, 1978) stemming from Birmingham Centre work evinces these continuing difficulties whilst offering detailed analysis of the BBC's *Nationwide*. In discussion of the use of personal pronouns in the programme, reference is made to certain characteristics which become, it is argued, 'at the level of the code, the site of complex ideological work'. However, this 'level', its relation to other linguistic or cultural levels and its possible internal differentiation are not issues taken up further in the research, although there are two or three subsequent references to various moments of encoding and decoding which do *suggest* a degree of differentiation.

Researchers have continued to tackle the problems of a general theory of codes in a number of ways, attempting to distinguish between code as system (s-code) and code as correlation (code) (Eco, 1976); between code as 'system of explicit social conventions' and hermeneutics as 'system of implicit, latent and purely contingent signs' (Guiraud, 1975) and endeavouring to redefine code in 'tighter' or 'looser' terms.[3]

---

[3] One recent move towards a 'loosening' can be discerned in Eco (1979). In an argument concerning the educational use of television, Eco notes that 'One is led to

Guiraud suggests a process by which 'looser' sign patterns acquire a consensual legitimacy and directness of reference to the point where they have 'the status of a technical code'.

Many uses of the term are almost metaphorical in that, rather than positing configurations at some linguistic level of organisation with attendant and important ideas of *predictability,* they suggest a conventional ordering 'of some sort' and serve to emphasise the fact that cultural meanings are achieved in relation to other cultural meanings as well as in relation to that which they express or refer to (a difficult area of theory, this) and therefore are not self-contained pairings of signifier and signified. Such a useful emphasis is, however, some way from the tenor of many research conclusions in semiotics, which do not show the hesitancy stemming from a sense of the limitations of the notion but instead imply regularised, plottable and predictable operations occurring with a considerable precision. In contrast to this, certain work exploring a general cultural semantics has made only guarded or limited use of the concept 'code'. In his early work, Barthes himself develops the idea of 'rhetoric' far more centrally and this, I think, permits him greater subtlety if also denying him the neat 'scientific' accuracies sought by others.

Goffman's *Frame Analysis* (1974) has an interesting footnote in which he refers to some diverse uses and connotations of 'code' in the course of discussing his choice of the not quite synonymous 'key' – on the whole, I believe, a more successful concept, if avowedly metaphoric in that it is a conscious *approximation* by reference to another, more fully known and grasped, condition or phenomenon. Work developing from Voloshinov's (1973) recently rediscovered notion of 'multi-accentuality' (the intersection, in signs, of differently oriented semantic

––––––––––

assume that under the umbrella term of codes and sub-codes, one is not only gathering something similar to the verbal, lexical or grammatical competence but also something more akin to rhetorical competence' (p. 19). He goes on to argue that 'rhetorical competence cannot be made explicit in the format of a set of grammatical rules but resides rather in the format of a storage of previous texts' (p. 19). From the context, it is clear that this is more an argument about the *acquisition* of competence than one about the possibilities for its *analysis* and I refer the reader to the article as a whole for an understanding of Eco's notion of the 'textual' as distinct from the 'grammatical'.

inflections stemming from different social positions of use) also seems to offer a valuable theorisation of differential social meaning, linking to some extent the problematics of semiology to those of one kind of sociolinguistics.

It is not, finally, the intention of this discussion paper to advocate the rejection of 'code' as a concept in cultural studies. It cannot be denied that the term has been used most frequently in some of the most exciting and suggestive work to be carried out in that broad area of inquiry. Here, Hall's papers over the past ten years constitute an outstanding example. What I think can be concluded is that many instances of its present use do not deliver what is promised and sometimes obscure what it is a prime intention of any cultural research to make clear – that is, how social meanings get made.

REFERENCES

Barthes, R. (1971). The rhetoric of the image, *Working Papers in Cultural Studies*, no. I, C.C.C.S., University of Birmingham. Translated by Brian Trench

Barthes, R. (1972). *Mythologies*, Jonathan Cape, London. Translated by Annette Lavers

Bateson, G. (1951). *Communication: the Social Matrix of Psychiatry*, The Norton Library, New York

Bernstein, B. (1971). Social class, language and socialisation, *Current Trends in Linguistics*, vol. 12, Mouton, The Hague

Brunsdon, C. and Morley, D. (1978). *Everyday Television: Nationwide*. B.F.I. monograph no. 10, London

Burgelin, O. (1972). Structural analysis and mass communications, in D. McQuail (ed.), *Sociology of Mass Communications*, Penguin, London

Camargo, M. de (1974). *The Ideological Dimension of Media Messages*, Stencilled occasional paper, C.C.C.S., University of Birmingham

Eco, U. (1972). Towards a semiotic inquiry into the television message, *Working Papers in Cultural Studies*, no. 6, C.C.C.S., University of Birmingham

Eco, U. (1976). *A Theory of Semiotics*, Indiana University Press, Indiana, USA

Eco, U. (1979). Can television teach? *Screen Education* no. 31, B.F.I., London

Geertz, C. (1973). *The Interpretation of Cultures*, Basic Books, New York

Goffman, E. (1974). *Frame Analysis*, Harper and Row, New York

Guiraud, P. (1975). *Semiology*, Routledge and Kegan Paul, London

Hall, S. (1972a). The social eye of *Picture Post*, *Working Papers in Cultural Studies*, no. 2, C.C.C.S., University of Birmingham

Hall, S. (1972*b*). The determinations of newsphotographs, *Working Papers in Cultural Studies*, no. 3, C.C.C.S., University of Birmingham

Hall, S. (1973). Encoding and decoding in the television discourse, Stencilled occasional paper, C.C.C.S., University of Birmingham

Hall, S. (1976). The 'unity' of current affairs television, *Working Papers in Cultural Studies*, no. 9, C.C.C.S., University of Birmingham (with I. Connell and L. Curti)

Hasan, R. (1973). Code, register and social dialect, in B. Bernstein (ed.), *Class, Codes and Control*, vol. 2, Routledge and Kegan Paul, London

Hawkes, T. (1977). *Structuralism and Semiotics*, Methuen, London

Leach, E. (1976). *Culture and Communication*, Cambridge University Press

Lévi-Strauss, C. (1963). *Structural Anthropology*, Basic Books, New York

Murdock, G. and Golding, P. (1977). Capitalism, Communication and Class Relations, in J. Curran *et al.* (eds), *Mass Communication and Society*, Edward Arnold, London

Parkin, F. (1971). *Class Inequality and Political Order*, MacGibbon and Kee, London

Shannon, C. and Weaver, W. (1949). *The Mathematical Theory of Communication*, Illinois University Press, Illinois

Voloshinov, V. N. (1973). *Marxism and the Philosophy of Language*, Seminar Press, New York

Wilden, A. (1972). *System and Structure*, Tavistock, London

Chapter 4

PRESUMPTION AS THEORY
'Realism' in Television Studies

———⊃⊂———

This polemical essay was written primarily as a result of the difficulties I had encountered in discussing 'realism' with students. In part, this was simply a reflection of the long-standing problems with using and debating the term which are evident in literary, theatrical and cinema criticism. But it also followed from the way the term had become caught up in the debate about 'ideology' from the late 1970s onwards, indicating a kind of mystification of power relations all the more effective in cinema and television for being conveyed through images. The illusory properties of the edited image were perceived to have a potency which made it the ideal vehicle for ideological communication.

I wanted to make a distinction which seemed fundamental to debates about realism but which was often concealed in contemporary debate – that between 'thematic realisms' (the relation of what a programme was about to reality) and 'formal realisms' (the way a programme achieved real-seemingness in its representation of the 'look' of the world). This is impossible to achieve tidily and the piece has some awkward moments, but the differentiation still seems to me to be important and under-acknowledged.

In suggesting polemically that 'realism' as an analytic term may be more trouble than it is worth, the piece also inclines towards the view that it is only in relation to fiction that the idea has value. To talk of the 'realism' of the news, or even of most kinds of documentary, is to move to a very different kind of argument about verisimilitude and veracity. To judge from the literature, this move is likely to confuse what is at issue even further.

In this note, I want to look at how the hectic history of ideas about television 'realism' has produced a situation whereby the very notion itself is close to being devoid of all useful analytical meaning. Whilst many critics and researchers continue to write as if a coherent theoretical corpus were indicated by the term, in my own teaching of television studies[1] it has increasingly seemed to require diagnosis rather than exposition. Following this, abandonment might turn out to be a better bet than attempted repair.

Realism and debates about its consequences lie close to the centre of 'television theory' (in a poststructuralist universe, an increasingly marooned assembly of ideas, stuck with the awkwardness of being at once more 'social' than cinema studies, more 'aesthetic' than media sociology, yet lacking the critical mass to break free of dependency on both).[2]

This centrality is not surprising since, of course, arguments about realism have also been central to criticism of cinema and, long before that, of dramatic and literary form.[3] Such arguments have a considerable degree of continuity in their concern with two factors – with the *pleasures* of realist forms (on the sources of this pleasure and perhaps on its aesthetic propriety) and with their *knowledge-effects* (involving assessment of their documentary and social analytic potential or, conversely, of their dangerous deceptiveness, whether viewed as naive or

[1] Despite the modest scope of what follows, I should like to acknowledge the usefulness of team-teaching a first-year course on television with John Thompson and Kay Richardson, my colleagues, and Karen Lury, a postgraduate student researching television aesthetics.

[2] The status and direction of 'television theory' has been critically commented on by John Caughie in a number of contexts, most recently in 'Adorno's reproach: repetition, difference and television genre', *Screen*, vol. 32, no. 2 (1991), pp. 127–53.

[3] I will mention here just three major source texts from the vast literature: Erich Auerbach's monumental *Mimesis: The Representation of Reality in Western Literature* (Princeton: Princeton University Press, 1953): Linda Nochlin's *Realism* (Harmondsworth: Penguin, 1971); and Christopher Williams's highly synthesised collection of edited extracts, *Realism and the Cinema* (London: Routledge, 1980).

strategic). However, a continuity of political/epistemological/aesthetic focus is also accompanied by disjunctions as the move is made from one medium to another. Broadcast television's institutional nature, generic order and modalities of viewing pose questions about text-reality relations in ways significantly different from either cinematic or literary forms, and although this difference has been recognised, there has been a failure to take the full measure of it theoretically. Instead, a loose generalism has ruled, by which 'realism' has come to be regarded (often ruefully) as television's defining aesthetic and social project – a view partly resulting from the unmonitored *expansion* of the notion, its proliferation into variants and its incorporation of television's expositional and journalistic forms.

The two issues around which debate has circulated with the most force and confusion might be tagged 'the real and the realistic', and 'realism of form/realism of theme'. Each involves problems of assumption, vagueness and diverse usage.

THE REAL AND THE REALISTIC

Clearly, film and television's capacities to render recorded visual likenesses of the physical world and to move a viewpoint through space mark the distinctive semantics of their 'realism'. They also serve to widen the gap between two different kinds of realist project. These might be called Realism 1 – the project of verisimilitude (of being *like* the real) and Realism 2 – the project of reference (of being *about* the real). In both cases, of course, 'the real' in question is at least partly a normative construction and disputable independently of any media representation. Later I want to discuss the gap between the two projects in terms of the broad categories of form and theme, but under the present heading I will concentrate on Realism 1 because this has been the area with which film and television theories of realism have primarily sought to engage. The aesthetic/technical/perceptual conditions of filmic/televisual verisimilitude and the frequent embedding of the latter in a simulacrum of the *physical* have generated widespread use of the idea that television realism is 'illusory' in effect. And it is with the use of this term that a first, general problem emerges. For debate about realism has often wanted to link an 'illusory' level of depictive form to a broader claim about the effectivity and deceptiveness of the 'knowledge' underlying, informing and conveyed by the depiction, a claim which television's socio-centrality attracts more strongly than cinema. Such a claim essentially assumes a passage from Realism 1 to Realism 2, whereby the seductive mechanisms of the former become the means and the accomplice of faulty understanding.

How can a passage of this kind be conceptualised as social action? Clearly, except for special cases (usually concerning very young children or the first arrival of television in non-modern cultures), viewers do *not* take what they see to be real *rather than* a depiction. What they *may* do is take it to be either a 'straight' imaging of the real (for instance, in news and documentary) thereby blocking questions about the nature of its *construction*, or an 'imaginatively convincing' piece of artifice (in a drama series, play or film), thereby perhaps investing *trust* in the reliability both of portrayed action and any general propositions inferred from the text. But these loose hypotheses, familiar enough in outline, involve a considerable speculative leap, for there has been too little serious attention paid by television studies to what on earth 'illusoriness' might point to in different generic contexts and what its place might be within the inter-dynamics of textuality, (re)cognition and social knowledge.

In a recent, illuminating attempt to reconceptualise the forms and processes of television around questions of repetition and difference, John Caughie cites Todorov on verisimilitude.[4] This quality, says Todorov, is the result of a text's conforming with generic norms in such a manner that it 'produces the *illusion* of realism'. But just how theoretically firm and useful is this statement? Cannot 'realism' be an acknowledged effect whose separation from (and discernible difference from) 'reality' forms part of its appreciation? And, on a slightly different reading, isn't such an awkward usage as the 'illusion of realism' dangerously close to either fusing together the realistic and the real (where, conventionally, the former has been seen as the illusion of the latter) or suggesting by implication the alternative of a 'real realism'? A sound general judgement here is that the idea of 'illusion' is a severely under-thought and over-extended one in television analysis, referring both to willed

---

[4] In Caughie, 'Adorno's reproach', p. 146. The quotation is from Tzvetan Todorov, *Introduction to Poetics* (Minneapolis: University of Minnesota Press, 1981), p. 18.

imaginative play and to deception in a manner which debilitates analysis of the medium's sociality.

Todorov is talking exclusively of fiction, of course. And this connects with a second major problem. For television theory has constituted itself largely by modified borrowings from film theory, where the 'realism' debate has been dominated by attention to the 'classic' realist forms of cinematic fiction. As a result, many contributions to television realist theory have been centred too firmly on the analysis of discrete, visually-led fictions to address television's generic and discursive pro-fusion and its range of non-diegetic (and often speech-led) relations with the 'real' (including those of its journalism).[5] As I suggested above, what is pointed to in (misguided) talk about the 'realism' of news and current-affairs television, and of interview-based documentary output, is essentially to do with *veracity of reference*, strategically underpinned by *veracities of image and speech*. In drama, it is far more likely to be matters of *verisimilitude* and of *plausibility* which are at stake. The fact of generic mix and generic innovation complicates, but does not yet displace, this basic discursive and epistemic difference.

REALISM AS FICTION: FORM AND THEME

I am arguing, then, that as a way of thinking about television depiction in general, 'realism' is very little more than a collection of begged questions. Even *within* the realm of television drama, however, the homeland of the idea, yet another major point of confusion bedevils usage. Resorting to the most basic terminology, this can be seen as one between realism(s) of form and realism(s) of theme. Realism of form has included conventions of staging, directing, acting, shooting and editing. Realism of theme obviously connects with the normative plausibility of characterisation, circumstance and action as well as being shaped within particular national and political pressures towards such categories as the 'socially ordinary', or the 'socially problematic' (often prescriptively inflected – what art *ought* to be about). The shift between these two ways of conceiving realism troubles many critical

---

[5] A recent counter to this tendency is to be found in the essays collected in Paddy Scannell (ed.), *Broadcast Talk* (London: Sage, 1991).

commentaries; producing either a straight conflation, or a tacking to and fro, or a complete ignoring of one side altogether.

Of the two, concern with realism of form has clearly been the dominant strand in the formation of television theory for the reason noted earlier – the influence of film theory. Moreover, this influence was exerted at a time (the mid-1970s) when the ideological consequences of classical Hollywood cinematic form constituted the key focus of a newly emerging radical wing of film studies. The precedents and possibilities of '*anti*-realism(s)' (drawing extensively on literary and theatrical parallels) was central to the cinematic debate.[6] However, in Britain, the use of documentary conventions in social or historical television drama gave rise to concurrent arguments of a rather different kind; about '*progressive* realism'. Formally, such 'progressiveness' was seen to be a function of a work's ability to open up at least *some* space for a critically distanced viewing within the larger framings of narrative continuity, even if these framings were not themselves brought into explicit question in the manner that cinematic radicalism recommended. What is interesting for my present argument is the extent to which this sub-debate[7] (of great significance within the development of television theory) involved the 'leaking-in' of positive ideas about 'realism of theme' as a counterpoint to negative ones about 'realism of form'. For nearly all of the British television dramas upon which discussion centred (the four-part series *Days of Hope*, screened by the BBC in 1975, attaining canonical status in this respect) depicted historical or contemporary events involving the politicisation of experience within the

[6] Among the critical overviews of this period, centrally involving *Screen*, is that to be found in Robert Lapsley and Michael Westlake, *Film Theory: An Introduction* (Manchester: Manchester University Press, 1988).

[7] The widely-cited exchange of views between Colin MacCabe and Colin McArthur provided an 'official' core to the debate. The relevant pieces, first published in *Screen* during 1975–6 and in the *Edinburgh TV Festival Magazine* 1977, are collected in edited form in Tony Bennett et al. (eds), *Popular Television and Film* (London: British Film Institute/Open University Press, 1981), pp. 305–18. Raymond Williams's 'A lecture on realism', *Screen*, vol. 18, no. 1 (1977), first delivered as a SEFT conference paper the previous year, was also influential. Though its overall conceptual scheme lacks sharpness, it is more comprehensively mindful of the political and aesthetic confusions attending debates about realism than most contemporary interventions.

British working class. This thematic (and publicly controversial) link between television representation and social and political realities needed to be addressed within a different analytic frame from that provided by the study of form, even if finally the two had to be related. Otherwise, the issue of 'reference' would be completely displaced by that of 'signification' – as often happened. An overblown notion of realism (partly parasitic on an overblown and increasingly mystical concept of ideology) acted as a block to any more incisive conceptualisation.[8]

REALISM AND THE POPULAR: GENRE AND AUDIENCE

In any account of 'realism's' troublesome career within cultural analysis, the long-standing, problematic relationship which the term has with 'naturalism' figures as an important sub-plot. In television criticism, both scholarly and journalistic, the two terms are routinely employed as synonyms, albeit with connotative nuances, though attempts are sometimes made to specify differentiation, and even contrast. 'Soft' versions of this make naturalism a kind of 'hi-fi' realism, as indicated above, whereas 'hard' versions tend to pick up on an influential strand of earlier socio-literary theory (particularly Lukács)[9] in distinguishing between a concern with physical detail and spatial and temporal norms on the one hand, and, on the other hand, a broader analytic, penetrative concern for essential 'truth'. Here again, we can see how that cruder division – between form and theme – seems always to be lurking suggestively in the background even where the explicit theorisation is more agile and ambitious.

With this in mind, I want to close with a reference to what seems to me to be the boldest recent attempt to clarify realism for television analysis. This is the one to be found in Chapter 1 of Ien Ang's *Watching*

[8] Terry Lovell's *Pictures of Reality* (London: British Film Institute, 1980) is a brilliantly suggestive account of this and related problems as they featured in British cultural studies at the end of the 1970s. Part of its originality lies in the way it is able to draw comparatively on the use made of 'realism' as a concept in sociological theory.

[9] Ernst Bloch et al. (eds), *Aesthetics and Politics* (London: New Left Books, 1978) contains key extracts from Brecht, Lukács, Adorno and Benjamin in a selection of 'debate' pieces whose reprinting provided an important stimulation and resource for literary and media studies argument.

Dallas.[10] Ang's commentary is driven by a 'demand-side' proposition, based on data from a viewer survey, that a central part of the pleasure which people take from *Dallas* (CBS/Lorimar, 1978–) is somehow derived from attributions of realism. The key question then becomes 'How does this attribution come to be made?' But having first posed realism as the key principle of television's popular aesthetic (an inductive move which a longer consideration of the book would do well to question), Ang proceeds to discuss both 'empirical realism' (likeness of setting, social action and ostensible theme) and 'classical realism' (formal conventions), only to find them both inadequate as explanations. It is finally 'emotional realism' (deep-level resonances with the emotional organisation of the viewer) which turns out to link text and experience in a way which fits the data. That this pioneering and conceptually reflexive study should find it necessary to stretch to a version of realism so rarified and disjunct from any formal or thematic criteria (and so uncertainly positioned in relation to that grand old non-realist idea, 'escapism') seems to me to be yet further evidence of the difficulties outlined above.

I have sketched out a view of 'realism' as a notion whose uncertainties have worked against clarity and development in television studies. These uncertainties principally concern questions about the psychological and epistemological character of the realist 'illusion', about the relation of fictional narratives to other dominant forms of television, and about the relation of forms to themes. We can be sure that *whatever* gets called 'realism' will be subject to historical and social contingency in respect of its formal conventions, its thematic choices and also those 'realities' against which both are appraised. But this does not exonerate us from the present requirement to think ourselves out of a mess.

[10] Ien Ang, *Watching Dallas* (London and New York: Methuen, 1985), pp. 13–50.

Chapter 5

CRITICISM AS SOCIOLOGY
Reading the Media

———⊃⊂———

This essay was written for an early 1980s volume, seeking a readership of literary scholars. It is particularly interested in the 'literary' origins of cultural studies and looks at the idea of 'reading' as a critical practice as it relates to the more sociological goals of media research. Having an interest on both sides of the slim line dividing socially-oriented literary studies from literary-oriented social studies, it still says something about the development of textual analysis which is missing from many other accounts. For instance, it notes the difference between analysing texts as the basis for a 'cultural archaeology', a dominant approach in what was then a developing strand of literary studies, and using them to predict influence, which became the principal goal of many media 'readings'. Less clearly, although I think suggestively, it also registers the broad difference between 'diagnostic' readings (in which textual indicators of varying directness are used to extrapolate to circumstances lying well beyond the realm of the text) and 'reconstructive' readings (in which a fuller sense of what the 'author meant' is the primary if not exclusive aim of close analysis).

———————

What kind of knowledge does criticism produce and how does it relate to enquiries which seek to promote historical or sociological rather than linguistic or aesthetic understanding? Posing these terms as alternatives might appear to ignore the ways in which concepts like culture and discourse have been employed to reject such distinctions. But how successful has this employment been at the level of research method?

In what follows, I want to pursue questions about criticism and social inquiry by looking at how critically-based approaches have been used to 'read' mass communications as part of 'reading culture'. I shall start by considering some conventional aims of literary analysis and by examining the assumptions of the first group of critics to take a close interest in media output. Following this, I want to discuss some methodological aspects of 'Cultural Studies' as it became formed from a line of socio-literary investigations then being importantly developed in the writings of Richard Hoggart and Raymond Williams.[1] In particular, I am interested in the problems involved, first, in attempting to read 'through' media material to originating conditions and contexts and then in attempting to read, as it were, 'ahead' of it, in such a way as to calculate its social influence.

THE CRITICAL APPROACH:
SOME ASSUMPTIONS AND INTENTIONS

When those self-conscious practices of interpretation which inform critical analysis are applied to texts defined as literary, the aim is most often that of heightening understanding, awareness and appreciation of the work's properties among a primarily academic readership. It is the work's own qualities as representation–cognitive and aesthetic – which provide the focus and object, as well as the primary ground, for exploration.

Despite the increase in recent years of more directly historical, social and political kinds of criticism, a majority of published studies and undergraduate programmes in literature are still based on a relationship to texts consonant with this broad goal of appreciation. In teaching, a strong implication of curriculum philosophy is that as well as there being literary pleasures to enjoy and much to learn *about* literature,

---

[1] Particularly Richard Hoggart, *The Uses of Literacy* (London, Chatto and Windus, 1957) and Raymond Williams, *The Long Revolution* (London, Chatto and Windus, 1961).

there is also much to learn *from* it, and that such knowledge of this kind accrues to the reader by virtue of the distinctive properties of authorial mind and sensibility evinced by the works themselves. In that regard, critical modes of knowing often operate partly within the terms of literary modes of knowing, this leading, understandably, to relations of reading in which there is a considerable deference exercised towards 'what the text knows and how it speaks' no matter what points of disapproval or disagreement are then taken up. Such an attitude may well be authentically the result of critical respect, though the very institutionalisation of the stance, and particularly its use in education, can serve to promote it as an obligatory formal/professional reading position. Many teachers of English will know how authoritarian appropriations and renderings of 'the canon' can push this through into what is finally a politically complicit narrowing of student reading possibilities and of attitudes to literary and social values.

Furthermore, one consequence of the related convention – that close interpretative analysis is an activity performable properly only on works considered to display distinguished qualities of mind (poor works being occasionally used to throw these qualities into relief) – is the automatic dismissal of critical attention to journalistic, broadcasting and popular cultural texts. This position remains powerful in many English departments, frequently blocking or marginalising work on popular fiction and on film and putting most of mass communication output beyond the pale altogether.

Now prejudice of this type is based on a mistaken sense of what most critically-informed work on the media is trying to do; assessments are made from too limited an idea of the aims of close reading. However, the way in which enquiries were carried out by those academics who contributed to the first major phase of critical interest in mass communication did not offer much by way of clear alternatives.

The most important of early critical engagements with modern media processes in Britain was that conducted during the 1930s by critics involved in the *Scrutiny* project, notably of course the Leavises.[2] Close readings here, when offered at all, were mostly used as illustrations

[2] See the general discussion and references in Francis Mulhern, *The Moment of Scrutiny* (London, New Left Books, 1979). A key text is F. R. Leavis and Denys Thompson, *Culture and Environment* (London, Chatto and Windus, 1932).

to support the general argument about mass culture. These readings provided what was really a secondary documentation of 'obvious' symptoms within what we may call a pathology of the modern. The primary evidence adduced to support the diagnosis (chronic debasement of public sensibility) consisted of generalised accounts of contemporary values and a selective and fanciful version of national cultural history.

With surprisingly little concern for differentiation, the output of the media was 'read off' against the aesthetic and moral criteria used in the appraisal of literature and not only found to be wanting but to constitute a threat to the values which literature (and criticism) stood for. It was not then thought necessary either to argue for this judgement with any sustained local emphasis or, indeed, given the judgement, to press further any specific enquiries into just how media forms and styles worked, in what ways they were read and what their registered pleasures might actually be. The critics are clearly aware of the way in which media language selectively assumes and advances particular social relationships and evaluations, but the connection with the cultural is made immediately, and then sustained, at the level of generalised adverse judgement. This stops the often penetrating sense of the increasing social centrality and commodification of media usages (particularly those of advertising) from being taken through into any kind of controlled social enquiry.

Here is an example of a suggestion for further work taken from Leavis and Thompson's *Culture and Environment*, published in 1933:

> Work out the life of a person who responds to the advertisements he or she reads. Compare it with the lives of the villagers in *Change in the Village* and of the Dodsons in *The Mill on the Floss*.[3]

At its worst, as this might imply, the *Scrutiny* perspective on the processes of the media carried an assumption about the practical consciousness of audiences and readerships so simplistic and brusquely unsympathetic (Q. D. Leavis's phrase 'the herd' remains disturbingly memorable)[4] as to preclude utterly the asking of the kinds of question I have indicated above.

[3] Leavis and Thompson, p. 113.
[4] Q. D. Leavis, *Fiction and the Reading Public* (London, Chatto and Windus, 1932). See p. 67 for example.

My interest here is not in taking up those important issues of cultural formation and change which the work of this group of critics raises but in noting the extent to which what was undertaken by them was primarily an evaluative polemic about the media and not an enquiry, least of all a detailed textual enquiry, into how media meanings were made. The one partial exception to this that I know of, though it concerns itself with popular fiction rather than 'the media' as such, is Q. D. Leavis's *Fiction and the Reading Public*.[5] Significantly, this too fails to enquire into the forms which popular readings of popular fiction take and instead assumes that the limitations detected in the texts answer to, or are reproduced as, limitations in the imagination of the readership.

Although from the 1930s onwards literary critics regularly commented on the character of media journalism and entertainment (sometimes with the doubtful aid of invented examples, so as to bring out what it was argued were the typical features of the kind of work under discussion) it was not until Birmingham University set up the Centre for Contemporary Cultural Studies in 1963 under the Directorship of Richard Hoggart that a more thorough debate about critical aims and methods began. Within the terms of the 'Cultural Studies' enterprise the idea of an enquiry into media texts became clearer and more easily separable from those principles and assumptions informing most of the work being done in literature departments. Although, as in the *Scrutiny* approach, the starting point was an anxiety about the increasing centrality of the media to modem society, the need for more fully descriptive and explanatory accounts replaced the earlier desire to set up as a sort of cultural magistrates' court through which the maximum number of decadent texts might receive a summary, critical come-uppance. It involved giving critical reading and the interpretative wholes which are its products ('readings') a much more developed sociological function.

CONTENT ANALYSIS AND THE
'CULTURAL READING'

When the literary-trained researchers of the Centre's first phase of activity considered what inroads Sociology had so far made on the

[5] Full reference above.

analysis of such material as newspapers, broadcast programmes and advertising copy they were not too impressed. In Britain, very little detailed attention had been given to media forms, styles and themes – the concentration of studies was in the social psychology of media influence – and most of the work that had been published followed the American social science tradition of 'content analysis'. This term refers to various procedures of textual study, all of which are based on the systematic categorisation and counting of content elements in a given media item.[6] The procedures permit a high degree of control over subjective impressionism at points in the analysis (though the initial phase of category formulation is clearly a vulnerable one), but their classifications are often unable to register the nuances of meaning at work in a given strip of imagery or verbal discourse. The breaking-up and classifying-out of texts into content categories works against any apprehension of the formal structures of the item, its local language use and the 'positionality', or significance in relation to one another and to the text as a whole, of the meanings generated.

What was abstracted from texts as either 'manifest' or (more trickily) as 'latent' content in these kinds of study, revealing though it might be about certain recurring thematic features in the material, seemed very far from those various sequences and organisations of significance which would be active in the assumptions and intentions of media producers and in the watching or reading experiences of audiences. In some research contexts, the very idea of 'content' study tended to under-rate or deny the idea of significant form, a tendency noticeable in the ease with which studies worked across formally quite different kinds of media material with an apparent confidence in the analytic constancy of the content categories employed.

Such limitations were regarded by many intending readers of culture not just as local problems of method but as aspects of a general conceptual inadequacy in the investigation of cultural practices by social scientists. The degree of reifying crudity, unimaginativeness and positivistic zeal ('sociological reductionism') frequently attributed to

[6] A critical and well-referenced account of early work is given in George Gerbner, 'On Content Analysis and Critical Research in Mass Communication', in Lewis Dexter and David White, eds, *People, Society and Mass Communications* (New York, The Free Press, 1963), pp. 476–500.

content studies seems exaggerated if the empirical boldness of many of the projects is allowed for, together with their nature as attempts to locate media items within existing, if unfortunately often functionalist, frameworks of social explanation.[7] Polemics of this kind also run the risk of downgrading the research benefits which highly explicit procedures of analysis can bring through replicability – that is to say, other people can check your findings.[8]

Nevertheless, many of the methods of content study then in use had been devised to advance the researching of a mass communication process modelled in diagrams as the sending of 'messages' to the public via the carriers of different 'channels' and 'formats'. This whole paradigm was rather disposed to regard the operation of the media within society as essentially the basic telegraph circuit writ large! Certainly, literary critics of whatever persuasion would have seen techniques so developed as unlikely to come up with anything about *Hamlet* they would find interesting. Cultural researchers had this at least in common with them, that they thought there was a good deal more going on in the images and the language they were looking at than any typology or system of classification had yet been able to account for.

Just such an attitude was clearly expressed by Alan Shuttleworth in one of the Centre's earliest discussion papers:

> This much is, I think, agreed within the Centre: that in order to undertake a sociology of literature, or a sociology of popular culture or the mass media, or a sociology of the history of taste, then only 'content analysis' of the same subtlety and discrimination is ade-

[7] A good case for the strengths of content analysis is made out in James Curran 'Content and Structuralist Analysis of Mass Communication', a paper prepared for Project Two of Course D305: Social Psychology (Milton Keynes, The Open University, 1976).

[8] For a discussion of how computer processing can be used to obtain inter-observer reliability see Alan Beardsworth, 'Analysing Press Content: Some Technical and Methodological Issues', in Harry Christian, ed., *The Sociology of Journalism and The Press* (University of Keele, Sociological Review Monograph 29, 1980), pp . 371–95. Much of the force of evidence in the Glasgow University Media Group's *Bad News* (London, Routledge and Kegan Paul, 1976) comes from procedures of this kind.

quate as would warrant a literary critical judgement. Here, clearly, is a task for the Centre: to train sociologists in literary criticism.[9]

Shuttleworth's main aim is to re-work Leavis's ideas about a 'humane centre' of studies[10] (importantly, studies whose primary if not exclusive method would be that of carrying out 'readings') so as to inform the more sociologically inclined enquiries underway at Birmingham. Given these new emphases though, how was that 'dense contact with particular material' which his paper claims criticism affords (and which contrasts with, but potentially complements, sociology's 'generalising modes of thought') to produce social knowledge? The initial answer followed on from a developing vein of work in literary studies by claiming that it provided the possibility of a sort of cultural 'depth analysis'. Unlike the abstracted categorisations of content analysis, a critical reading well done – closeness permitting depth – could, it was argued, interpret and diagnose back down the line of semantic links and shifts connecting textual rhetorics and their components with the matrices of meaning in cultural and social organisation.

READING AS CULTURAL ARCHAEOLOGY

It might be useful here to consider three comments by Richard Hoggart in order to bring out some general principles of this 'depth analysis' and to aid a discussion of the problems which attend an extension of critical concerns in this direction. The first comes from *The Uses of Literacy* (1957), the other two from a book review written in 1967:

[We] have to try to see beyond the habits to what the habits stand for, to see through the statements to what the statements really mean (which may be the opposite of the statements themselves),

---

[9] Alan Shuttleworth, 'A Humane Centre', in *Occasional Papers Two* (University of Birmingham, 1966), reprinted in Peter Davison *et al.*, eds, *Literary Taste, Culture and Mass Communication* XIV (Cambridge, Chadwyck-Healey, 1980), pp. 43–66.

[10] See the arguments in F. R. Leavis, *Education and The University* (London, Cambridge University Press, second edition, 1979).

to detect the differing pressures of emotion behind idiomatic phrases and ritualistic observances.[11]

That method [of the book under review] is primarily to look at the texts themselves and work out their cultural meanings, the degree to which they express the consciousness of the age below the explicit level, at the level where the strains show.[12]

We are making, in a sense very difficult to define satisfactorily, a reading for values, one which brings to the surface the complex patterns of values embodied in, carried by, the prose.[13]

While all three of these comments might be regarded as being about the same broad socially interpretative project, I think it is interesting to note how the first one differs in emphasis from the other two. They all suggest a kind of reading work which is diagnostic rather than reconstructive (in the sense that they want to get from their texts something other than what these texts appear to be saying 'officially') but the first formulation proposes this primarily as an activity of contextualisation. It is more a kind of broad reading than a close reading that is proposed. Here, the interpretative work of the analyst/reader is directed towards locating the items within hypothesised or assumed schemes of social significance, thus rendering them diagnosable. These schemes have to be already analytically available (at least in provisional ways) in order that recognition and correlation (what stands for what, what is really being said, etc.) can be accomplished. What can then be observed about the utterances or behaviours lies 'beyond', 'through' or 'behind' the signifying forms themselves and, indeed, is presumably not routinely perceivable via the kinds of interpretations that would be performed on them in everyday life. It is worth pointing out here though that, of course, unless the analyst has access to the schemes used to produce such quotidian interpretations, any inferences as to 'real' significance

---

[11] Hoggart, *The Uses of Literacy*, p. 18. Quoted by Stuart Hall in the Introduction to *Working Papers in Cultural Studies 1* (Birmingham University, Centre for Contemporary Cultural Studies, 1971, p. 7.

[12] Richard Hoggart, 'On Cultural Analysis', in *Speaking to Each Other*, vol. I: *About Society* (London, Penguin, 1973), p. 120.

[13] Hoggart, 'On Cultural Analysis', p. 121.

are likely to be impaired by an inadequate construing of the 'apparent'.

The other two quotations appear to pose the relationship between analyst/reader, text and interpretative context rather differently. Here, in addition to that narrative or informational sense which is the first objective of reconstructive reading (literary readings may also reconstruct an implied propositional sense which, as a characteristic of art discourse, is deemed 'official'), the texts are seen to be carrying or 'embodying' certain social meanings and values. It is the analyst/reader's job to make these explicit by an intimate apprehension of forms and tones (they have to be brought 'to the surface'). However, despite this emphasis on the texts as sources (and, as such, the points of focus of what are viewed as enquiries primarily conducted upon and within texts), connections with the earlier kind of reading outlined are present. In the second quotation a key part of the project is the calculation of the extent to which the works examined express 'the consciousness of the age'. This phrase, an odd one to find in Hoggart's critical vocabulary, is clearly something of a throwback to the grand monolithic abstractions of one kind of literary history. Be that as it may, the putative historical entity it refers to is something which the analyst must be expected to have knowledge of prior to the analysis if he or she is to assess the text's expression of it. While this does not by itself condemn the procedure described to circularity, a dialectical movement between generalities and the particular being necessary to all knowledge production, it does suggest, as I think do the differences across the three formulations, certain difficulties presented by 'deep reading' as a method no matter what kind of material is under scrutiny. Cultural analysts have themselves registered these difficulties[14] and in recent years the employment of semiotic concepts, replacing Hoggart's tentative phrasings with theories about the operation of socio-textual codes, has posed them in new ways. However, they remain as problems for any reading-based enquiry and have been particularly apparent in studies of the media, notwithstanding the many illuminating investigations of discursive form which have been carried out.

[14]An interesting account of methodological issues attending the 'deep reading' of literature is given in Andrew Tolson, 'Reading Literature as Culture', *Working Papers in Cultural Studies* 4 (1974), pp. 51–68.

They follow, I believe, from the relations existing in any piece of 'cultural reading' between what can be referred to, developing my remarks on the quotations, as its textualist and contextualist phases, and from the nature of these phases as produced in the analysis.

In the textualist phase, the material (news item, advertisement, television programme etc.) seems to be located within the analysis as some multi-levelled *repository* of meaning, having a deep level or 'deep structures' (Chomsky's phrase does extensive duty here) to which the reading can penetrate. These meanings are perceived to be properties of the texts even though they do not form part of its 'official' discourse and may not be registered in the settings of lay interpretation (e.g. reading the paper, watching television, seeing the hoarding from the bus). To use a phrase from one kind of deterministic account, they are 'inscribed' within the textual form, an impress of its sociality as a product, and can be retrieved by sensitive analysis. The line of historical and social enquiry thus lies 'down and through' the text.

In the contextualist phase, which in many media analyses is given prefatory and/or concluding functions and occupies a relatively small part of the account, the researcher frames and situates the texts (as read, or about to be read, 'closely') thus making them mean within the terms of what are consciously applied, and perhaps explicitly argued for, orders of significance. This is most clearly seen to occur at very general levels of diagnostic reading (e.g. certain editions of *Picture Post* located within the contexts both of photo-journalism's development and British social history[15]). What is 'read off' here is registered (as it would have to be in Hoggart's first example above) not as a property of the texts but as a product of the descriptive/explanatory orders themselves as they engage with and organise into significance symptomatic features of the material under analysis. These orders may, of course, be held to identify and account for factors (assumptions, inferences, elements of what Williams, in a still useful if troublesome phrase, terms 'structures of feeling') which are active in the production practices of media employees and in the interpretations made by audiences, whether consciously in use here or not.

---

[15] The example is drawn from Stuart Hall, 'The Social Eye of the Picture Post', *Working Papers in Cultural Studies* 2 (1972), pp. 71–120. This study is a very general contextualising account with suggestions for more detailed textual analyses.

Now the separability of the actual processes from which these two phases are constructed seems to me to be less clear a matter than cultural readings customarily require in order to provide warrant for the propositions they wish to make from textual study. Indeed, the textualist phase can be viewed as involving an analytically convenient objectification, a complex semantic entity being produced from the physical fact and separateness of units of image, speech and notation – that programme, this article. However temporarily, it threatens to leave out of account the constitutive function of interpretative schemes – whether reconstructive or diagnostic, lay or academic in intention – for all realisation of significance from notational form. Newspaper articles, advertisements, documentaries, comedy shows – like novels, poems and plays – gain what referential and expressive stability they have by virtue of those conventions of significance within which image and notation become meaning and by virtue of the alignments between these conventions across social groupings, situations and time. This much is a grounding principle of cultural analysis. It is precisely to those conventions less directly entailed by the more determinate language features, to conventions of assumption, implication and connotation, including those involving sense-making from still and moving images, layout styles and narrative sequences, that 'deep readings' of the media most often seek to address themselves. To do this by posing the text as somehow a 'frozen moment' in the circulation of public values and significance, a held layering of meanings indexical to the culture at large and susceptible of semantic excavation, is to ignore interpretative contingency in the interests of securing a handy data base.

One typical result of this is the reproduction in the sphere of cultural analysis of familiar critical arguments about textual 'presence'.[16] One researcher finds evidence ('traces' perhaps) in the text of, say, conflicting production aims or certain (possibly historically distant) ideological

---

[16] Some of these problems are documented in Graham Murdock and Peter Golding 'Ideology and the Mass Media: The Question of Determination', in Michèle Barratt *et al.*, eds, *Ideology and Cultural Production* (London, Croom Helm, 1979), pp. 198–224. See also D. Anderson and W. Sharrock, 'Biassing the News: Technical Issues in Media Studies', *Sociology* XIII, iii (1979), pp. 368–85 and the subsequent responses in issues XIV, iii and XIV, iv (1980).

themes or reportorial assumptions which cannot be 'found' by other researchers. We might, for instance, have an argument about what was 'in' and what was 'not in' television coverage of the Falklands War. Many contested characteristics (e.g. omissions and recurrences of names, phrases, explanations, descriptions and shots; formal features of the discourse) might be confidently established purely by textual reference. But a whole range of propositions which it would be important for cultural analysts to make about active assumptions and meanings could not be sustained, as might well be attempted, by textual reference alone, however tightly theorised the readings. An 'is it there or not?' framing (which in literary studies can be made to fit in happily with the idea of the text as kaleidoscopic promoter of possibilities) is a misplaced and potentially over-assertive way of handling an enquiry where the question is not 'how can this text be read?' but 'what were the organising values, inferences and assumptions within which it was produced?'.

Clearly, the status and relationships of texts and readings confront every student of expressive forms with difficult problems of conceptualisation. Nevertheless, the kind of enquiry which the last question above points to – properly one part of a pragmatics of media discourse – can only be conducted by the linking of an analytic focus upon textual forms with a much wider range of inter-textual, ethnographic and historical investigations into public orders of significance. The schemes of interpretation at work at different phases of the production and circulation of media texts would here be a central point of concern, one which included sharper reflexive awareness of schemes brought into play by the analyst.

This is not to allot texts a merely relative importance as simply projections of interpretative schemes. Questions of textual notation and the kinds of significance that can be generated from this cannot be handled in terms of a single, unitary 'meaning' of which either the text or the reader must then be identified as the real source.[17] Nor is it to suggest that some sort of reversal of 'deep reading' emphases is what is required were it achievable, texts (old radio comedy programmes, for

---

[17] Useful discussions of these matters as they affect literary studies are collected in S. Suleiman and I. Crosman, eds, *The Reader in the Text* (Princeton, Princeton University Press, 1980).

instance) somehow being realised into their full, 'deep' social indexicality when externally researched interpretative schemes were applied.

Indeed, no easy prescriptions for research can be made, but more use of oral history methods, interviews, related non-media texts and cross-textual comparisons could, it seems to me, provide 'thicker' interpretative accounts to connect both with analytic readings and with institutional studies. Such an extended programme of work would present the researcher with new kinds of interpretative and correlational opportunities, a lot more of them than at present in media institutions and on production phases.

In fact, an early Birmingham Centre study of the popular press and social change, published in 1974 as *Paper Voices*,[18] is brilliantly suggestive about the connections that can be made between a variously sourced history of particular public attitudes and feelings and the specific shifts in a newspaper's mode of address and editorial position. Disappointingly, it remains itself under-documented outside of its main sections of textual commentary.

I have suggested, then, that contrary to the ambitions of textual depth analysis, the social character of what the media produce is not something to which 'readings' can give privileged access. This applies equally to those projects which have concerned themselves less with matters of origin and formation than with questions of influence.

READING AND CULTURAL INFLUENCE

In attempting to go 'through' texts to local and general conditions of production, media readings are close in approaches and problems (specifically, those following from assumptions about textual stability and held meanings) to that kind of literary historiography suggested by Raymond Williams in his early and influential outline study of the 1840s.[19] However, the second objective which analytic reading was given within cultural research on the media has no parallel in literary studies at all. This involved the carrying forward of a textual interpretation into

[18] A. C. H. Smith, *Paper Voices* (London, Chatto and Windus, 1975). See particularly the Introduction by Stuart Hall.
[19] Williams, *The Long Revolution*, chapter 2.

arguments about the significance media items had for contemporary media publics and about their influential powers.

In literary studies, the discursive protocols of criticism certainly do not require that offered interpretations be capable of being shared by or attributable to readers at large, let alone be indicative of influence exerted upon them. This is because literary studies are addressed to a professional community of skilled readers within which originality of personal interpretation, plausibly argued from consensually agreeable textual properties, is what a reading conventionally delivers. Of course, some of the texts which form the corpus of literary study are read, if at all, by only a very few people outside the framings and requirements of academic work, so that questions about their public meanings and their effects upon general consciousness are unlikely to be raised. But even where the works enjoy a wider circulation, their general reader-ship is not considered of much importance to the pursuit of critical knowledge. *Wuthering Heights*, for instance, is read widely in library editions and paperback form outside of schools, colleges and universities but the collections of essays and the conference papers which analyse it have little place for any study or attempted survey of its particular significances, pleasures and appeals within the broader sphere of its public existence. Research of this kind might even be regarded as evidencing some new manifestation of the affective fallacy. The inter-pretations, then, which the book receives from non-professional readers in settings other than a syllabus do not count in a critical enterprise which holds the text as provisionally free of any specific production or reception determinants in order to promote readings linking textual potential with highly distinctive kinds of, as it were, 'creative insight'.

Some studies of media work, particularly those on film and on broadcast drama, have reproduced this critical stance almost without modification, although in film studies there has lately been discussion about the extent to which a form of cultural analysis rather than a form of criticism should be the main business in hand.[20]

Certainly, as we have already seen, the social research objectives of the cultural reading make its interpretative task a different one. Here once again, but now with respect to what happens 'in front' of the text,

---

[20] An excellent, polemical discussion is John Hill's 'Ideology, Economy and the British Cinema', in Barrett, *Ideology and Cultural Production*, pp. 112–34.

it is precisely not originality that is sought but a descriptive reconstruction of the kinds of meanings, evaluations and ideological clusterings which make their reinforcing or modifying entry into the sphere of public discourse with each particular media narrative, news item, magazine article, television commercial and so on.

This returns the researcher to a similar set of problems, of textualism and contextualism, to those which I have outlined above. For just as texts themselves do not have an independent deep semantics sufficient to provide primary data for the reconstruction of a history and a context, neither can their variable public realisations by different viewers and readers in different settings be established through close analysis.

As one moves further away from the more socially objective significance of descriptive language, through conventions of cultural inference and on to the imaginings of character and action elicited by visual and verbal narratives (all unhelpfully subsumed into 'the text's meaning' by some commentators) so the analyst's own textual realisations become increasingly inadequate as bases for general accounts. This is so whether the readings are somehow consciously 'offset' to try and allow for the interpretative tendencies of kinds of ideal typical reader or projected straight from the analyst's version on to an undifferentiated public understanding and response, as in the accounts given by the *Scrutiny* group. The differentiating factors of class, education, gender, age and personal biography work to multiply the public existences of a text (whether *Coronation Street*, *Boys from the Blackstuff*, the editorials of the *Daily Mirror* or *News at Ten*) out of the comprehensive possession of any attempted 'normative' reading.

Among the variations of registered significance there is clearly much common interpretative and imaginative activity going on. As well as being constructed within broadly available conventions of language, imagery and cultural association, media texts are constructed within the terms of social power relations. Particular established and developing ways of organising social perception, dominant ways of framing and explaining social structure and action are at work. We can say of these that they are implicit in the texts (as 'preferred readings', to use an influential research notion) but the prepositional metaphor of this phrasing should not be allowed to lead to assumptions about their presence there – awaiting the analyst's discovery – somehow independent of the reading work by which they come to mean. Perhaps ideas of completeness attaching to the widely used notion 'cultural product' are unhelpful here.

Many of the most interesting readings of contemporary media material have worked because they offer detailed descriptions of the reading or viewing experience – commentaries on their own realisations – 'read off' from the social sense of an analyst sufficiently inside common interpretative frames for the account to seem to answer to a much wider sustaining of meanings.[21] This kind of phenomenological study necessarily remains suggestive and highly variable, however, as a means for assessing the public 'take up' of media productions. Further enquiry here, as in the study of production contexts, can only proceed through a more comprehensive attention to the heterogeneity of interpretative schemes and practices in social use. And this is to raise only the question of understood meanings and significance, in relation to which any questions of influence and attitude formation would have to be carefully posed.

Again, as I suggested earlier, the need is for ethnographic data on audiences and readerships to place alongside and to support and inform the textual studies. Methodologically bold though this work may have to be initially, the availability of more accounts and transcripts concerning what sense media publics make of what they see and hear and how they make it is a necessity for the development of a textual sociology.

The most important work so far undertaken in this area is undoubtedly that by David Morley, on audiences for the early evening television news magazine *Nationwide*.[22] This complements an analytic reading of the programme by detailed discussion with members of different audience groups. One of the many difficulties of method it encounters is that of getting adequate access to the primary work of audience interpretation as this follows the programme's sequence of face-to-camera presentation, links, interviews and voiced-over filmed reports. Study of the subsequent expressions of viewer reaction, including those of disagreement with propositional content, is no substitute for more fundamental examination of the processes by which the media

[21] For instance, on popular television, Richard Dyer, 'The Meaning of Tom Jones', *Working Papers in Cultural Studies 1* (1971), pp. 53–64. A similar success principle may be at work in Roland Barthes, *Mythologies* (tr. A. Lavers, London, Cape, 1972).

[22] David Morley, The 'Nationwide' Audience (London, British Film Institute, 1980).

significations are construed. There are signs that Morley's initiative is now getting the critical attention and development which it deserves and that attempts to follow through empirical enquiries into the inter-acting levels of sense-making from media items will be one part of this.[23]

Proper analytic address to the schemes of significance and to the contingencies upon which the social existence of media meanings depend must involve more wide-ranging and developed types of work on interpretational settings. These might include working across the phases of production and reception of a single item or programme, carrying out more extensive intertextual studies, and doing interview surveys around public issues which are receiving a variety of media treatments in different genres and forms.[24]

This is a large undertaking, and interpretative or linguistic readings will play an important analytical role in it. They will not, however, constitute an attempt to derive from textual criticism some kind of social hermeneutics. The cultural cannot be reconstructed by extrapolation either backwards or forwards out of the textual because it is just what is at issue in deciding what texts are and mean.

[23] See Justin Wren-Lewis, 'The Encoding/Decoding Model: Criticisms and Redevelopments for Research on Decoding', *Media, Culture and Society* V, ii (1983), pp. 179–97.

[24] Some elements of this broader approach are impressively present in Phillip Elliott, Graham Murdock and Philip Schlesinger, '"Terrorism" and The State: A Case Study of the Discourses of Television', *Media, Culture and Society* V, ii (1983), pp. 155–77.

Chapter 6

WHY STUDY MEDIA FORM?

The close study of form is an essential element of student work on the media, developing a more precise sense of image, sound and word usage. It is also an important aspect of research, although in some areas – the study of depictions of violence is the one I choose here – it has not figured as strongly as it might. I wanted to make the case for formal study by relating it to ideas of 'content' and 'influence', whilst also admitting the extent to which an overly-elaborate analytic jargon had become an obstacle to comprehension and progress.

In this chapter I shall look at why the study of form is of key importance in any programme of media studies or, for that matter, of media research. This aim will require some attention to be paid to definitions of 'form' (notoriously, in relation to 'content') and also to ideas about its analysis and to the way in which it is linked with other dimensions or 'moments' in the whole process of mediation. I shall attempt to give the discussion exemplification and grounding by taking one area in which factors of form, for long overlooked, are now being recognised in their full complexity and importance – representations of violence on television.

It is significant for my argument and examples, and for the evaluation and use of them by student readers, that the range of media studies and communication studies available in the UK and mainland Europe shows considerable variation in the scale and kind of attention given to formal analysis. On some courses, particularly those influenced strongly by arts and humanities perspectives, elements drawn from linguistic study are clearly seen as 'core'. On other courses, particularly those generated from a social studies base, such attention may be far less extensive, with few if any opportunities for going beyond a basic awareness. These variations are often a proper reflection of staff specialisations but they also indicate a tension within the whole field of media studies, a tension between humanities and social science modes of inquiry and, at bottom, what I have elsewhere (Corner 1995) described as a tension between media studies as a form of 'criticism' (where the primary emphasis may be given to media output) and media studies as a form of 'sociology' (where primary emphasis may be given to history, institutions, production practices and audiences). I do not hold the view that the tension is an irresolvable one or (a different point) that it is necessarily unproductive as a play-off of one kind of approach against another. However, I do think that *one* way in which media studies might develop and progress is by more sustained dia-logue between contributing disciplines precisely on issues to do with media form and its interconnection with media production and consumption.

Another good reason for giving formal issues close attention in any course of study is that both in broadcasting and the press there have recently been quite radical changes in form, occasioned by the stronger market need for mediations, as commodities, to appeal to specific viewers and audiences. A key process here has been that of 'hybridis-ation', the mixing of elements from what were previously distinct conventions, thus breaking down some of the older genres, including those dividing off 'higher' from 'lower' forms or demarcating the 'serious' from the 'entertaining'. A quick walk around the magazine racks of a High Street newsagent will show how this has affected the specialist publications sector, with its various and often strident attempts to construct a readership subculture around particular hobbies and interests which have either newly emerged or which have undergone radical change. In broadcasting, one international shift has been towards a new kind of 'reality programme', drawing on documentary formats and dramatic techniques to provide thrilling stories of real-life action (see the overview in Kilborn 1994).

It is perhaps worth noting, as a final preliminary, that from the point of view of many teachers and researchers, media studies has already suffered from an overdose of inquiry into 'form' (the term formal*ism* has quite a long history as a label for distortion and limitation, especially in relation to literary and fine arts scholarship). I have some sympathy with this view, but I would want to argue that the problem, rather than deriving from formal analysis as such, lies with the way in which it has often been done.

My basic claim about the study of form is that only by attending to formal issues can we engage with two things which it is necessary for media studies to tackle. The first of these is the range of ways in which the media industries are engaged in the production of cultural artefacts, 'made things', whether these are 'fictional' or 'factual' by categorisation. The second is that any understanding of 'media influence', actual or potential, will come to grief if it is not sensitive to this artefactual character and to the way it is instrumental in cueing those various acts of knowing and feeling – of finding sense and significance and having emotions – which happen in us when we read newspapers, watch television and listen to radio.

FORM AND CONTENT

By 'form' I mean the particular organisations of signification which constitute a given item *as communication*, for instance, an advertising hoarding, an episode of a situation comedy on television, an article in the local evening newspaper. Inevitably, such signification is *conventional*, drawing on what may well be a large and complex range of conventions for doing what it tries to do and for being what it is. These conventions will inform word choice and syntax (as for instance in a popular newspaper's editorial column), and they will be behind the ways in which a particular image is lit and photographed and the items which are depicted in it are composed within a given frame and perspective (as for instance in an advertising hoarding). Even if the communication is designed to read, sound or look highly 'original', conventions of form will be an important constitutive element (perhaps informing decisions about what is omitted or what is done with a significant difference). The basic 'content' of any communication could, in most cases, be articulated by the use of any one of a number of different formal choices. So, for instance, there exists an extremely wide range of English syntactical and lexical variations by which to tell someone in one sentence that you wish them to shut the door through which they have just entered. And there exists a similarly wide range of visual techniques and styles by which to shoot, for the opening of a television programme, the main waterfront buildings of Liverpool. On the other side of the equation, the formal means used in telling people to shut doors and in depicting Liverpool will have a relative independence from their employment in these particular instances. Following the two different lines of possibility thus opened up is, in fact, a key feature of formal analysis – *noting how this instance might have been communicated differently and noting how different instances have been communicated similarly*.

One objection to what I have said so far might come from someone firmly committed to the view that it is impossible to separate 'form' from 'content', with the implication that even to use these terms at all is to slip into self-deception. This seems to me to be an overreaction to those analysts who have gone on about 'form' without any apparent regard at all for 'content' and those who have studied 'content' without paying the slightest attention to 'form'. Certainly, we can agree that any study should connect with *both*, but it is quite legitimate (indeed, absolutely necessary to analytic progress) to see the two as separate, if only the better to understand the way in which they are tightly interconnected. Media analysts have a rather bad track record of claiming the *fusion* of things which, illogically, they also wish to claim are *related* (only separate things can relate!). To make this point about separation clearer, take my own specialism. I have a particular academic interest in documentary film and television, its history and development. In pursuing this, I believe that I can analyse documentaries in a meaningful way while paying primary attention to their particular visual and aural 'shape' and their use of distinctive mediating devices rather than to their content (see, for instance, Corner 1996b). Their content may well be the factor which most directly 'sells' them to an audience (a documentary about drug abuse, for instance, connecting with different expectations, interests and fears from a documentary about the growth of the sport of rock-climbing). However, I am inquiring into the kinds of 'communicational packages' that modern documentaries are, and this is not at all a topic-specific inquiry, even though one of the interesting things in it may well be to see how similar formal systems are modified when they are applied to different substantive themes.

What about the reverse case? Is it possible as a viewer to take the 'content' of a documentary without regard to the form? This question poses the difference between analytic attention to a communication and 'normal' attention. For while it is certainly possible to watch and enjoy a documentary without consciously registering much if anything to do with its communicative design (this is in fact the intended and normative way in which most documentaries *are* watched), the 'content' is made available to meaningful consciousness only *through* the form, so the form is 'at work' even though the viewer (perhaps especially when the viewer) is unaware of it. This complicates the form – content relationship: content, like form, is still a 'separable' element but in any given media artefact it has a high level of form dependency – *it is rendered through the form*. At certain levels of (high) generality, its separability *may* be relatively trouble free for the conduct of an argument (for example, the number of appearances in British television drama of Black police officers in comparison with Black criminals). Elsewhere, abstraction of content may be hazardous (for example, in discussing the frequency of depiction of acts of murder on television – where, as I shall argue later, the matter of the form of depiction is absolutely vital to what is at issue).

So, to summarise, my view is that while content and form indicate elements of communication which cannot usefully be considered in *isolation* from each other – in many instances the interconnections and dependencies are too close for that – they are analytically separable and, indeed, the consequences of their not being so would be extremely dire for media analysis. Certain studies of the media rightly place emphasis on content factors; others are more interested in questions of communicative design and construction. Although there is some truth in the charge that attention to form has sometimes failed to get to grips with the *political and social consequences* of mediation, preferring instead to speculate about the complexities of signification, there is a long history of mass communication research which has rendered itself of limited value by its inattention to the details of language and depiction, to the *means* by which communication gets done. Despite some of the theoretical obscurities it has had a habit of falling into, one of the principal and continuing contributions of 'cultural studies' to international media research has been its refusal to foreclose on what, at the cost of sounding very un-social scientific, we might call the

'mysteries' of signification. It has always tried to remember that mediation is a matter of *symbolic exchange*. In fact, this exchange is, judged
from one point of view, very one-sided. The media put out symbols and
audiences and readerships 'receive' them. However, this is to miss the
point that audiences and readerships invest their own symbolic
resources (their ways of attaching meaning and value to, for instance,
word, image, narrative and character) in coming to terms with media
productions they encounter, enjoying some of them, disliking some
and quite possibly not 'getting the sense' of quite a few too. This leads
on to the links between form and interpretation.

FORM AND INTERPRETATION

Other chapters in this book refer in more detail to the ways in which
study of the variables of interpretation has figured in recent media
inquiry. A realisation of the extent to which 'meaning' is contingent
upon the act of interpretation rather than being a property somehow
inherent to media artefacts themselves, simply projected outwards
from them, has been the single most important point of development
in recent media research. It has given rise to a number of challenging
lines of study into the social conditions of interpretability as they vary
among different readerships and audiences. It has also broken forever
any 'direct' linkage between media items and influence, since it has
introduced variables of meaning into the research perspective. Research
on influence has always been aware of the importance of variables but
it has generally related these to a 'message' whose basic meaning was
stable even if the 'use' made of it or its 'trigger' function in prompting
behaviour were not. I have written on these issues elsewhere (Corner
1996a) and, indeed, there is continuing debate over just what the
implications of interpretation are for *any* theory of influence.

The scope of the debate exceeds this chapter's remit but what I
would want to claim here is that an emphasis on the 'role of the reader'
in giving meaning to what they see and hear in no way reduces the
need for media research to pay attention to questions of signification.
Far from it. We shall understand meaning-making 'from' the media as
a social process only if we increase our understanding of significatory
structures and their operation within the 'spaces and times' of media
texts (both written and broadcast forms have spatial and temporal

dimensions to their communicative character). Signification also needs to be traced back to specific authorial/editorial/technical production practices too, many of which are self-consciously rhetorical in the sense that they intend to cause certain kinds of response in the viewer or reader (think, for instance, of the 'formal' properties required of photographs which are placed on the cover of outdoor sports magazines, what they are supposed to 'say' about the exhilaration and intensity of skiing, surfing or rock-climbing quite apart from their literal depiction of a sporting act).

The scope of readers/viewers to interpret variably is, in any given case, constrained by the social and biographical factors informing the interpretative framework they mobilise in response to a mediated item. A fanatical surfer will 'read' a shot of a big wave differently from someone who hates the sea, for instance. Someone who has been an unemployed machinist for four years may well understand a television news item on job centres differently from someone who is a successful banker. But interpretative limitations are not the only constraint. The significations themselves carry levels of determination which it would be extremely odd to find varying greatly in their interpretative 'uptake'. At the most obvious level, this is sustained by the social stability of signs themselves. If the news item I mentioned above finished with a shot of individuals shaking their head as they looked at the 'jobs available' board and then leaving the job centre promptly, the visual cues of this little narrativisation would be hard not to interpret as indicating a *problem* – an undersupply of jobs – whatever information was carried elsewhere in the story. If the reporter went as far as to run a voice-over across this scene, along the lines 'But disappointment still awaits many who call here', it would be virtually impossible to imagine much interpretative latitude among viewers (although there would definitely be differences in social and political response, including the possibility of complaints being made to the broadcasters on grounds of bias). If we take the case of the picture of the big wave, the cultural connotations of waves with 'power' is securely enough established in our culture (reinforced as it is by advertising and packaging) to generate that reading for most viewers of the image, whatever their interest in, or experience of, the sea. Of course, the dedicated surfer may be able, at a quick glance, to place the image into a numerical category of wave power potential!

This general point needs making lest media artefacts end up being seen as kinds of open invitations to create 'individual' meanings. 'Individual' meanings *are* created around media artefacts, and *all* meanings have to be *attributed* to artefacts by those who apprehend them. But meanings are attributed in response to powerful *signifiers*, whose job it is precisely to direct and organise meaning-making, to generate sense and significance and as far as possible to cue feelings too. It is hardly surprising that, when it comes to discussing last night's news, film or comedy, we have a lot of meanings to *share* as well as to discuss, debate and perhaps contest.

ELEMENTS OF FORMAL ANALYSIS

Analysis of communicative form has been undertaken in a wide range of disciplines; literary criticism, linguistics and art history have lengthy traditions of inquiry while film studies, cultural sociology, cultural studies and media studies have more recent bodies of work. One of the key factors differentiating the analytic approaches is their level of systematic formulation, that is the degree to which they self-consciously follow procedures. Many literary critics analysing a poem, for instance, will do so with extremely close attention to its linguistic character, but probably with little by way of procedural explicitness. Linguists, on the other hand, often analyse language with careful regard to their own analytic schemes and its categories, which are made explicit in the analysis. Such a difference is partly a product of the different *aims* of inquiry – in the one case an artistic appreciation, in the other a description of language structures – but many types of communicative analyses combine a number of aims, so distinctions of this kind can prove troublesome. Semiotics, the science of signs developed by Ferdinand de Saussure in the early part of the twentieth century, has undoubtedly seemed to many to offer the most general and rigorous system for analysing communication – its emphasis on structural interrelations providing a kind of linguistic framework for use across a whole range of different media forms. Here, the work of Roland Barthes (especially 1972) has been exemplary and highly influential (in media studies, Fiske and Hartley 1978 was a key text). However, the very precision of semiotics has been a problem in so far as it is grounded in too rigid a sense of communicative order (assuming, for instance, a high degree of non-changeability in sign-meanings) and in a frequent ignoring of that process of interpretation, described above, by which meaning is the product of acts of reading and viewing.

Despite some excellent and suggestive work, semiotics has by no means consolidated itself as the dominant perspective on formal analysis it once appeared well on the way to becoming. Another problem here has been that of visual analysis. Clearly, the study of visual depiction, whether in drawing, photography, film, television or whatever, requires different tools from the study of written and spoken language (see Messaris 1994). With language, the signifying units of words and the rules of combination (syntax) may not be immutable but they do have a degree of significatory stability. A dictionary and a grammar primer are (imperfect) indications of this. The units and combinatory rules of, say, photography are far harder to grasp as a formal system. For a start, in a photograph we have no obvious signifying unit to compare with the word. Second, we face the problem that while a sentence is clearly a communicative device capable of generating all sorts of propositional and evaluative information, a photograph of, say, a car in a street may just seem to be saying – 'a car in the street'. In other words, it may appear to have no communicative project apart from presenting a 'likeness'. Barthes's (1977) insightful discussion of the photograph as appearing to be 'a message without a code' takes up this very point. We may recognise that there is *more* communicative work going on than this, and that indeed the 'message' is 'coded', but specifying the visual code system and its particular local application has proved, not surprisingly, to be a formidable and controversial task.

All I will say here on this major question is that any serious project of formal analysis must have reasonably consistent, and preferably explicit, criteria for *identifying* distinctive components of communication. It must have a way of providing a *description* of communicative organisation which registers these components in rule-based combination (the rules cannot be 100 per cent tight but they must show good consistency across instances). The project should then be able to offer *explanations* which are able to address the link between particular significatory elements and relative stabilities in socially ascribed meaning. It should, in short, be able to match 'sign' to 'sense'.

Say, for instance, I wanted to look at how elements from 'camcorder culture' had become inscribed within mainstream media output (which they have, in advertising and a range of documentary and magazine programmes). I would need to identify those elements, their combination across a range of instances with other elements, and the kinds of social meaning which they were designed to generate (some clues as to intentions here might be got from contexts of use). Of course, it could turn out that rather different aspects of 'camcorderism' (e.g. authenticity, domesticity, ineptness, expectations of comedy) were being deployed and that analysis needed to move to a *typology* of usage, indicating the range of variants and their associated formal properties. As I noted earlier, ignoring specific 'content' here is likely to lead to elaborate speculation, the subsequent value of which may be very questionable. Alertness to form in relation to specific themes and contexts (and perhaps to production practices and/or the sampled responses of viewers) might make useful headway into charting how the terms of mainstream televisuality are now being modified by non-professional practice.

There is a great deal more to be said about formal analysis at the level of theory and method. However, having drawn attention to at least some of the issues, I want to look at how much of what I have noted so far in this chapter comes to bear on one particular area of concern – screen violence.

THE SCREEN VIOLENCE ISSUE

The issue of 'screen violence' has generated much debate in recent years, both in respect of feature films and of broadcast television. Fears of a negative connection between depictions of violence and real behaviour have been widely expressed, and at the time of writing, the whole issue is being aired again in relation to the availability of the 'V chip', which allows parents electronically to limit the range of material which their children can view. Generally speaking, there have been three kinds of fear. First, there has been fear of depicted violence stimulating real violence. Second, there has been fear of depicted violence reducing sensitivity and proper concern for real violence. Third, there has been fear of depicted violence inducing excessive and unwarranted levels of anxiety among sections of the population about being the victims of violence. However, the first two kinds of fear occur most frequently in the UK, and they have been developed in respect of both fictional and non-fictional material, with particular attention being paid to the vulnerability of young viewers.

Elsewhere (Corner 1995) I have explored some of the broader issues surrounding 'screen violence', including the basic cultural paradox that forms of behaviour which are widely considered to be wrong in reality constitute the basis of quite a wide range of popular culture. It is necessary, I believe, for analysis to come to terms with the widespread *enjoyment* of depicted violence (violence as 'play') across most age-groups and social groups before much progress can be made on the question. In order to do this, in my earlier writing I used the terms 'turn-on' and 'turn-off' violence to indicate two basic ways in which depictions might differ. In 'turn-off' depictions (and the portrayals of most serious TV drama would fit here, as would the majority of violent incidents in soap operas), the aim is to portray the violence within terms of the moral framings of everyday life, so that a degree of unpleasantness, disturbance and even distress will accompany the viewing (directors have to be careful here, *too* much distress might bring a problem for the viewers and then for the broadcasters and the regulating authorities). In 'turn on' depictions by contrast (and a whole range of popular drama formats, including thrillers and many 'cop shows' would fit here) the aim is to portray violence in a way which provides excitement by heightened action, intensified character performance and, perhaps, by spectacular visual effects. Of course, even allowing for the difficulty of applying my categories with consistency and precision, it is quite possible for an item to shift between 'turn-off' and 'turn-on' depictions. In fact, it seems pretty clear that a number of recent films structure this shift into their basic design, often giving rise to a debate about their moral ambivalence.

But it should be immediately obvious how quickly this whole debate turns into a set of questions about *form*, and cannot be properly addressed using items of extracted *content*. So, for instance, it is almost (not entirely) beside the point to note how many murders there are each week on network television. What we need to know is the dramatic context for the incidents and the ways in which the murders were portrayed, since it is clear that a murder done in a certain way on television can leave the viewer relatively unmoved whereas a lower-level act of violence, like repeated blows to the body, can be deeply disturbing but can also be exciting or even comic.

On the basis of these general points, we might formulate a rule along the following lines – the more that violence which is judged to be 'turn on' involves sustained, graphic depiction of physical injury, the more worry is likely to be generated around it. We could even go further – the more that this violence lacks obvious action-values (chases, fights, etc.) and therefore depends on the violence itself to generate viewing intensity, the more likely it is that it will be judged controversial.

As I shall indicate, these 'rules' tend to hide some considerable complexities, but they do seem close to the ones which have been applied in recent years, particularly in relation to the newer stylisations of, and preoccupations with, violence to be found in cinema. What specific questions of form do they raise, and how is form related to the particular psychology of viewing, with its broader cultural interconnections, which comes into play when watching violent depictions?

We might initially work with a checklist of factors which, in combination, could be seen to constitute key features of depiction. On it, we would need such items as:

- Strength of prior identification with characters (both those to whom violence is done and those who are violent).
- Links within the narrative to notions of justness and unjustness in relation to specific violent events. The indication of general and local causation would be important here. Clearly, war films tend to have a radically different structure from crime films, which nevertheless vary among themselves.
- The levels of 'realism' (themselves posing well-attested problems of definition) and of 'entertainment' at work within the surrounding narrative. Themes and characterisation would in part reflect these levels.
- The terms in which the violent scene was *acted*; for instance, expressions of pleasure and of pain, the relationships established between act and persons.
- The terms in which the violent scene was *shot* and *edited*; for instance, proximities to action, camera angles, camera mobility and variable viewpoints, duration of shots, explicit indications of physical injury. The presence, and type, of sounds and music on soundtrack.

Such a list might quickly enable us to make important differentiations.

For instance, scenes designed to have a turn-off effect will not usually be accompanied by an exciting musical score. And that kind of cartoon violence and old-style western violence which (while clearly 'turn-on') appears not to bother many people will have nothing like the degree of explicit indications of injury of more recent productions. We might wonder why 'sanitisation' of this kind is thought so culturally accept-able! However, at other points the scheme would be challenged and perhaps even thrown into question. Just *how* subjective in significance are the workings of the various formal factors which are under review? It is certainly possible for someone to find a scene intended as 'turn-off' to work as 'turn-on' (this comes up frequently when directors defend themselves against a 'turn-on' charge) and the reverse is true too, but how varied, for instance, are our thresholds for judging 'comic violence' and what adjustments to depiction can make acceptable the previously unacceptable and vice versa?

Here, it would be useful to have the means to produce depictions designed precisely to test depictive factors with sample audiences. A much-cited study (Docherty 1990), although it could not run to this, had respondents do editing and sequence work on scripts containing violent scenes, observing how (simulated) 'producerly' criteria related to the 'consumerly' ones normally used in discussion of responses. In the process, it identified a number of areas of tension and potential conflict in people's relation to the 'violent'.

All these procedures of analysis have limitations on their reliability. But they take us to the heart of this vexed issue, raising questions about culture, imagination and fantasy – as well as about attitudes and behaviour – much more quickly than is achieved by holding up a set of moral norms against statistics showing the frequency of certain depicted acts.

THE FUTURE OF FORM IN MEDIA STUDY

This has been no more than a brief opening-up of some questions about media form and its study. Students using this book will probably be doing concurrent work on a range of specific issues involving form and the various questions it poses (for instance, in advertising, televi-sion drama, news and current affairs, popular press reporting and feature cinema). I have wanted to stand back a little and address the matter directly at a general level. My fundamental argument is that symbolic exchange is the pivotal moment in mass communication processes, the moment around which both production capacities and intentions and consumer expectations and interpretations gather. If media systems exert power, then it is primarily through the mediations which appear on page and screen (and, by implication, through the absence of those which do not) that this is exercised. To this process, form is central and it is therefore a factor in consideration of media history, media institutions, media policy and media audiences.

The analysis of form poses problems for the analyst, and some work has slipped into obscurity and inconsequentiality, but this is no good reason for displacing attention on to other factors which are thought to present themselves more securely as objects of study. Given its pivotal position in mediation, we need to engage with its complexities as directly as we can.

REFERENCES

Barthes, R. (1972) *Mythologies*, London: Jonathan Cape.

Barthes, R. (1977) 'The rhetoric of the image', in R. Barthes, *Image-Music-Text*, London: Fontana.

Corner, J. (1995) *Television Form and Public Address*, London: Arnold.

Corner, J. (1996a) 'Reappraising reception: theories, concepts and methods', in J. Curran and M. Gurevitch (eds) *Mass Media and Society*, 2nd edn, London: Arnold.

Corner, J. (1996b) *The Art of Record*, Manchester: Manchester University Press.

Docherty, D. (1990) *Violence in TV Fiction* (BSC Annual Review), London: Broadcasting Standards Council.

Fiske, J. and Hartley, J. (1978) *Reading Television*, London: Methuen.

Kilborn, R. (1994) 'How real can you get: recent developments in "reality television"', *European Journal of Communication* 9(4): 421–39.

Messaris, P. (1994) *Visual Literacy: Image, Mind and Reality*, Boulder, CO: Westview.

Chapter 7

MEANING, GENRE AND CONTEXT
The Problematics of
'Public Knowledge' in the
New Audience Studies

———— ❯❮ ————

In 1991, I took up an invitation by James Curran and Michael Gurevitch to write a critical overview of 'reception studies'. It followed a decade of work on audiences, greatly inspired by the work of David Morley but also drawing on a number of other important studies, including those by Ien Ang and Janice Radway. My feeling was that this strand of work was in danger of losing its sense of direction and was in need of conceptual and methodological reappraisal, being prone among other things to a number of confusions around the notions of 'reading', 'interpretation' and 'decoding'.

The piece became more widely and positively cited than I had expected. An interest in critical stock-taking was starting to be felt internationally.

David Morley (Television Audiences and Cultural Studies, London: Routledge, 1992) has since observed that the contrast I set up between 'macro' and 'micro' perspectives, and the relation to power which each is seen to entail, runs the risk of implicitly privileging older, cruder approaches to ideology and of not recognising the importance of a situated analysis of the 'domestic' and the 'personal'. I accept this, although I would still hold to my view that much audience research was in danger of abandoning the search for power relations rather than simply shifting it on to other territory.

My observations about meaning are only pointers towards a more developed and precise account of interpretative process, not a firm alternative to the 'decoding' model. Although there continues to be valuable inquiry undertaken, I think the area is still characterised by conceptual drift and uncertainty about aims which only further critical revision will correct.

As other articles in this collection will variously indicate, one of the most striking points of development in the media research of the last decade has centred upon questions of 'reception'. These questions have essentially been ones about *what* meanings audiences make of what they see, hear and read, *why* these meanings rather than others are produced by specific audiences from the range of interpretative possibilities, and *how* these activities of meaning-making, located as they usually are in the settings of everyday domestic life, might relate to ideas about the power of the media and about the constitution of public knowledge, sentiment and values.

Such a development – in many ways a return to the empirical study of audiences with a new and sharper agenda concerning the nature of meaning as social action – has rightly been seen (Curran 1990) to have exerted a 'revisionary' pull on those theories about media power which were grounded in structuralist accounts of ideology and which were so highly influential in British research in the 1970s (see, for instance, Hall 1977 for a critical review from within the perspective). So much so that in some 'new paradigm' work concerned with reception, the question of an ideological level of media processes, or indeed of media power as a political issue *at all*, has slipped almost entirely off the main research agenda, if not from framing commentary. In what *might* turn out finally to be a temporary phase of 'high swing' on the pendulum, so much conceptual effort has been centred on audiences' interpretative activity that even the preliminary theorisation of influence has become *awkward*. There have been a number of useful overviews of 'reception' studies recently (for instance, Schroder 1987, Morley 1989, Ang 1990, Jensen 1990a, Moores 1990) along with a consideration of their ethnographic methods (see the special issues of the *Journal of Communication Inquiry* 13.2. 1989 and *Cultural Studies* 4.1. 1990).

My interest in this chapter is not in offering a further synoptic account but in bringing as pointedly into focus as I can what I see to be three key areas both of conceptual emphasis and of conceptual difficulty for the new enterprise. These point outwards towards more general problems for the theorising and analysis of cultural power. Since my own interests are focused on the relationship between broadcast journalism and public knowledge, I shall pursue my argument with this primarily in mind, in the awareness that other aspects of the 'new wave' audience study to which I shall occasionally refer, most prominently those concerned with popular drama series, are dealt with in detail elsewhere in the present volume.

The three broad areas which I have selected are best indicated by the terms 'meaning', 'genre' and 'context'. Around each one, it seems to me, there has clustered not only a number of conflicting accounts but also confusions. One of the results of this is that although overviewing commentators may talk boldly of a thriving new 'ethnographic' tradition (in a not uncontested reference to the conventions of 'in-depth' anthropological data gathering), there is in fact a good deal of deconstructive work to be done if significant further progress is to be made. It also seems to me that the three terms are now employed in two rather distinct kinds of project, posing the 'influence/interpretation' question in different ways.

One project is concerned primarily with the media as an agency of public knowledge and 'definitional' power, with a focus on news and current affairs output and a direct connection with the politics of information and the viewer as citizen (illustrative examples here would be Morley 1980, Lewis 1985, Jensen 1986, Dahlgren 1988, Hoijer 1990, Corner, Richardson and Fenton 1990a and 1990b). The recent researches of Danish, Swedish and Norwegian scholars in the area now constitute a highly-focused and intensively theorised strand of this line of enquiry, which can conveniently be called the *public knowledge* project.

The other project is concerned primarily with the implications for social consciousness of the media as a source of entertainment and is thereby connected with the social problematics of 'taste' and of pleasure (for instance, those concerning class and gender) within industrialised popular culture. This we can call the *popular culture* project (illustrative examples would be Ang 1985, parts of Morley 1986, and Seiter et al.

1989, with Radway 1984 offering a pioneering and influential study of the reading of popular literature).

I do not mean to suggest that the two projects have no interconnection. Clearly, to fail to recognise the aesthetic character, narrative organisation and broad cultural embedding of news and current affairs exposition or the social knowledges and classificatory systems at work in popular drama, would be to work with a crassly simplistic idea of what is going on. Researchers have shown themselves to be fully aware of this (see for instance Liebes and Katz 1990, and Livingstone 1988 on the cognitive dimension of popular series drama). Yet a divergence along the lines suggested, in research problematics and the terms thought appropriate to addressing them (variously weighted towards aesthetic, psychological, sociological or directly political theorisation) seems not only to be clearly discernible but to be increasing. One sign of this is the extent to which recent overviews of the area reference a different literature, allowing for a number of common, 'core' texts, according to their chosen perspective. Under my three headings I shall comment further on the nature and consequence of this divergence.

Some questions might also be asked about the general *political* relations at work (by default or otherwise) in the sudden bourgeoning of 'demand-side' research (both on fictional and non-fictional forms) from the mid 1980s onwards. In certain versions of the reception perspective, this seems to have amounted to a form of sociological quietism, or loss of critical energy, in which increasing emphasis on the micro-processes of viewing relations displaces (though rarely explicitly so) an engagement with the macro-structures of media and society. In other versions, mostly within the 'popular culture' project, a celebratory tone has sometimes appeared, the academic critic enthusiastically validating the choices of entertainment made by 'ordinary viewers' in a way which then prompts fundamental questions about the aims both of aesthetic and of social inquiry. (The hugely influential Fiske 1987 carries some of these tones, though he is a good deal more circumspect about the macro framings of economic and cultural power than many commentators have given credit for.) A Norwegian scholar, Jostein Gripsrud, has noted some further possible consequences of the tendency:

By pretending that the academic critic's pleasure is the same as anybody else's, s/he not only erases the socio-cultural differences

between the academic and the genre's core audiences, but also
avoids analyzing the specificities of, for instance, the film scholar's
pleasures in soap-watching. (Gripsrud 1989, p. 198)

At a more general level, the widespread interest in reception issues
seems to connect closely, and not co-incidentally, with certain aspects
of the turn towards Postmodernism which several arts and social science
disciplines have recently taken. This turn, too complex in character to
summarise here, has often signalled what might be judged, according
to viewpoint, as either as a 'sophistication' or a 'softening' of the terms
of cultural critique. A heightened sense of ambivalence towards the
artefacts and pleasures produced by the resources and market inven-
tiveness of the Late Capitalist culture industries has been displayed at
the very same time as it has become fashionable to be elaborately
nervous about ideas of truth, reason and power (see the excellent
synoptic account of these matters in Harvey 1989).

Under my chosen headings, I shall open out discussion on these
and other points as well as on those more specifically to do with the
significatory and social relations of sense-making, with the *pragmatics*
of mediation.[1]

First of all, however, it might be useful, before looking in detail at
its *problems*, if I were to state as succinctly as possible the broad terms
of 'reception research' as I perceive them within the perspective of my
own interest in the production of public knowledge. Though much of
what I say has relevance for work on other than TV audiences, it is
upon TV that most studies have focused and, as a result, my own
discussion is often pulled into having a medium-specific character.

There is no doubt that David Morley's *The 'Nationwide' Audience*
(1980) represents the single most significant publication in the emergence of the reception perspective in British research. Based on group-
discussions following the video screening of an early evening news
magazine, it set up an agenda about 'text–viewer' relations, interpretative variation and 'knowing through television' which has been a major
influence. It is also the case that his *Family Television* (1986), in which a
number of families are interviewed in depth about their viewing habits
and pleasures, was a further, important contribution. This second book
showed a shift of emphasis from the plotting of specific, social correlations of text/viewer/meaning to a broad study of domestic settings and

patterns of use. As I shall argue later, such a shift is not without its problems, particularly if regarded straightforwardly as a 'development' out of the earlier work.

The first of these studies, and those by other researchers which are indebted to it (few of those published over the last decade are not), can be seen as partly a reaction against two aspects of the contemporary state of theory and research. First of all, a reaction against the (often structuralist) 'textualism' of cultural studies in Britain. There had been an attempt within this strand of work to develop semiotics into a 'science of the text' whereby not only could a precise and 'deep' textual meaning be discerned by close reading, but also the 'ideological effect' a text would promote in viewers could be predicted by assessment of the positioning force it exerted upon receptive acts (see Corner 1985 for an historical tracing of these ideas in Cultural Studies). Morley's work was an attempt to break out from the formalism of this position into a more open engagement with the variables and complexities of 'meaning-in-process'.

Secondly, the relative neglect of 'meaning' in favour of 'function' and 'use' in contemporary empirical audience research was identified and reacted to (though the 'naivety' of early research on this score can be exaggerated; see Curran 1990). The form which 're-conceptualisation' took here involved an attempt to carry over cultural studies' alertness to discursive and symbolic processes into an analysis of the organisation and forms of viewing activities rather than those of media texts themselves. 'Influence', whatever its strength and direction, had to work through meaning, and it was to the formal and social complexity of meaning-production that the new research addressed itself. Meaning was seen as *intra-textual* (requiring analysis of textual structures), *inter-textual* (requiring analysis, among other things, of genres and relations between them) but also finally and decisively *interpretative* (requiring research into the situated practice of 'receptive' understanding).

The method, both in *The 'Nationwide' Audience* and in the sizeable number of research projects to follow Morley's lead, was quite directly to generate group talk about television following specially arranged screenings. Through such data, 'readings' (for ethnography, despite its interest in viewers' accounts, could not dispense with the need for analyst interpretation) might be made of the way in which the talk indicated patterns of variation in the meanings-for-the-viewer. These patterns might then be connected with other factors differentiating the individual viewers or viewing groups questioned. In other words, not only *variation* but also *the reasons for it and the consequences of it* might, if only in part, be accessible.

The overall general significance attributed to this work within media studies (a matter not without 'reception research' possibilities itself!) was towards seeing the variations in response as indicating a revision *downwards* in hypotheses about media power (to some extent, replicating the shifts in emphasis of an earlier chapter in media research history; see Curran 1990). Forms of interpretative 'resistance', as this was indicated in Morley's use of the terms 'negotiated' and 'oppositional' to classify types of non-aligned reading position, were seen to be more widespread than 'subordination' (the reproduction of 'dominant' meanings) and, as I have indicated earlier, a number of commentators welcomed the newly-recognised degree of viewer and reader 'independence' which this was presumed to document. It should be noted here, however, that Morley himself has never failed to emphasise in his work the extent to which cultural power and ideological reproduction work as much, if not more, through the social factors bearing upon interpretative action as they do through that which might be thought to be 'carried' by, or 'inscribed' within, media texts themselves. Failure to attend properly to this has often led to a situation in which an overly simplistic play-off between textual power and reader freedom, with a variety of possible 'truce' positions mooted, has been implicit in debate (see the extensive and polemical treatment by a number of authors in *Critical Studies in Mass Communication 5* (1988) pp. 217–54.

I want now to turn to the first of the three areas which I have suggested merit closer, critical attention.

1 MEANING

Quite what a given critic or researcher wishes to include within the term 'meaning' in now-familiar phrases like 'the viewer constructs the meaning of the programme' or 'the text is capable of producing many different meanings', or 'this is the meaning to which you are guided by the text' is nowhere near as clear as it might be. This lack of clarity has hindered the development of productive critical dialogue between researchers and it has made for a situation in which, whilst there are a lot of (rather repetitive) profundities around concerning meaning and the media, there is a chronically under-theorised sense of what precisely is at issue.

Although spatial metaphors have to be used cautiously in investigating semantic and pragmatic processes, the notion of 'levels' can, I believe, offer some preliminary differentiations here and thereby help to highlight some of the pitfalls of too casual a usage. In many uses of 'meaning', three different levels of meaning can be seen to be indicated, often collapsed together. These are:

1. A level at which a word, image or sequence's primary significa-
    tion is recognised and comprehended (e.g. the written word
    'typewriter', the spoken word 'violence', a shot of a baby in a
    pushchair, a TV car chase). This recognition and comprehension
    will, of course, take account of, or be responsive to, those sur-
    rounding and concurrent factors which add up to a *context of use*
    (the theoretical establishment of which in any research design
    presents a major problem – see below). With due regard for
    problems of category borderlines, for many purposes this level
    can still be usefully thought of, following classic early semiotics,
    as relating to the level of 'denotation'.
2. A level at which a word, image or sequence's secondary, implica-
    tory, or associative signification is recognised and comprehended.
    This level will vary according to the character either of the signifier
    or the signified or a combination of both (i.e. named or visually
    depicted entities will vary in their degree of symbolic/metaphoric
    resonance – a shot of a chair may have less than a shot of a cruise
    missile – and so will named abstractions like 'politeness' or
    'death'). Clearly, the secondary signifying force of each verbal
    phrasing or articulation of image will be dependent in part not
    only on its local elements but on their organisation within the
    larger textual unit which is being attended to. At this secondary
    level, the effect of variations in the resources upon which viewers
    draw to make sense of and to evaluate their viewing will be
    greater than at the primary level, where the grounding of inter-
    pretative work is in more broadly consensual sign-forms and
    conventions. A *biographical* as well as a *social* variable may start
    to figure more strongly in the organising of perceptual, cogni-
    tive and significance-according activity. The term 'connotation'

continues to be useful to indicate the level of signification involved here, though it has too often been thought of exclusively in terms either of the 'emotive' or of the associations generated by visual images. Moreover, many applications of the denotation/connotation distinction are woefully simplistic and rigid.[2]

3. A level at which viewers and readers attach a generalised significance to what they have seen and heard, evaluating it (perhaps in relation to its perceived presuppositions and entailments if it has propositional force) and locating it within a negotiated place in their knowledge or memory, where it may continue to do modifying work on other constituents of their consciousness (and, indeed, of their unconscious). When some researchers talk of the 'response' or of 'the reading' which a particular media artefact elicited, it is clearly to this level which they are most often referring. The widely-used idea of 'preferred reading' to indicate a weighting of significations in a text towards one ideologically-aligned understanding of it also relates most directly to this level (Morley 1980 is a seminal application). Although the concept of 'preferred reading' signalled a welcome move away from 'hard' notions of textual power (the general significance 'encoded' need not be the one 'decoded') and towards the influence/interpretation interface, its use really remained limited to news and current affairs texts, particularly those in which declaredly neutral discourses were in fact organised in terms of systematically 'weighted' categories and relationships. Even here, in addressing the long-standing problematics of journalism's professed objectivity, slippage across different levels of meaning is evident. In a study of the cultural and political consequences of the popular press, James Curran and Colin Sparks develop a useful discussion of just how obstructive this slippage can be to a conceptualisation of media power (Curran and Sparks 1991), a point I return to below.

In engaging with this level of 'response', a general distinction between factual and fictional or entertainment-based texts needs to be retained. In the former, the viewer is often drawn quite directly into a 'response' which involves relations of belief and disbelief, agreement and disagreement. The kinds of text-processing which viewers perform in the two cases are likely to be quite

distinctive. Morley (1980) is, again, the seminal instance of agree-
ment/disagreement variation being plotted in respondent talk.

For the purposes of an investigation into the interaction between
media forms and audiences, it seems a good idea to keep some such
three-tier differentiation in mind, perhaps theorising it more tightly and
with a less impressionistic vocabulary, in relation *both* to significatory
forms and their interpretative processing (see the useful attempt in
Lewis 1985). This might act not only against the terminology of mechanistic unity ('decoding') but also against loose generalisation. In a
recent and shrewd account of current research issues, Peter Dahlgren
(1988) appears to fall temporary victim to this tendency when he notes:

> By 'meaning' I refer here to the processes of making sense of the
> world around us. It has to do with creating a general coherence in
> our lives, of establishing an order in which to anchor our existence.
> (p. 287)

This is certainly true but by no means is it enough.

To illustrate the clear need for differentiation in analytic practice, we
can take the example of two people who meet at work the morning
after the broadcasting of a television play which both saw. They discuss
the play and quite soon a difference of judgement emerges about the
ending, which one person thought moving and the other silly. How far
is this difference actually one of assessments being made of the same
set of meanings? How far are evaluative criteria and their application
really at issue? It might well be that further debate uncovers the fact
that they have divergent notions of what was actually 'going on' in
the ending. We could even imagine a situation where, after one of
them has persuasively put the case to the other about just what *was*
happening in the last scene, there is now agreement that, indeed, it
was a moving and apt conclusion. There is a further twist we can give
to this imaginary circumstance. Let us say that right from start the
two agree that the play and its ending were impressive. Does this
guarantee that they have a shared version of its meaning? No. It is
perfectly possible (though perhaps less likely than the first scenario)
that there are radical divergences in their sense of what it all meant or
what key parts of it meant. And if the conversation gets intense enough
for detailed appraisals to be offered, such divergence may become

apparent and put a halt to their mutual appreciation, shifting it into debate and dispute.

Having suggested that a 'levels' model of meaning may be useful to hang on to and refine, despite problems if the typology becomes over-rigid, I want now to note two particular difficulties which then immediately arise and require attention (since they are usually disguised by the failure, right from the start, to register differentiation). We can call one of them the *linearity problem*, the other the *part-whole problem*.

The linearity problem follows from regarding the different levels of meaning (either in my crude typology or any refined variant) as somehow activated *in a sequence of separate moments* (the spatial metaphor tends to slide analysts into thinking this way). Thus, the viewer accords primary meaning, then secondary meaning, then significance, in a phased process. Clearly, this will not do. Anticipations of significance work to guide the registration of secondary and the organisation of primary meaning right from the start of a stretch of viewing or reading activity. As a programme or article unfolds within transmission-time or reading-time, a developing structure of anticipation and possibilities, together with the specific inter-textual connections and evaluations made by readers or viewers, bears 'downwards' on the reading at the same time as there is also a generative process 'upwards' from primary signification through into a generalised significance. This inter-articulation of sense-making practices, ranging from the basic construing of words and images through to the making of propositional, thematic and/ or fictive-imaginary understandings and assessments, is a continuous, self-modifying 'loop' process rather than anything working through distinct and separate phases. It is also, thereby, a process which is saturated *culturally* throughout, though to rather different degrees and effect at different points. (On the 'incremental' character of this process see Lewis 1983 and the social psychology perspective of Hoijer 1990. Reception research as a whole could benefit from a firmer engagement with the kind of issues raised in recent 'text comprehension' literature, despite its behavioural orientation. See, for instance, Bradac (ed.) 1989.)

The part-whole problem is a related issue. For as well as meaning-making requiring a movement 'upwards' from the recognition of, for instance, colours, shapes and sounds to the attributing of significance, there is also a movement 'outwards' from the interpretation of localised signifiers to an ongoing entity which is seen finally to be the expressive whole (the advert, the play, the news item, etc). And just as the 'upward' movement is accompanied by the 'downward' process of realising new primary meanings within generalised framings, so this movement 'outwards' is accompanied by an 'inwards' movement locating elements, perhaps retrospectively, within the emerging organisation of the pro-gramme/text and its broader inter-textuality. This duality presents a challenge to researchers, who require to engage with its dynamics, not slip into using established categories and divisions.

Although I have done little more than raise some questions and perhaps suggest both the necessity and the awkwardness of coming to closer terms with the phenomena under study, I want to leave this account of meaning by drawing out some of its principal implications for current theorising around texts and readers.

The main implication concerns the extent to which, and the manner in which, 'openness' and variation in meaning are regarded as aspects of text–reader relations. For the extensive use of the term 'polysemy' (see Fiske 1987) to indicate the richness of meaning possibilities in media texts has tended to suggest an indeterminacy *only* closed down by interpretative action (even if this action *is* seen to be one shaped within the terms of the cultural system rather than being an act of 'free choice'). In part, this may be the result of theoretical observations about the polysemy of individual signs when considered in abstract being transferred over to observations about their use within textual structures. In the latter situation the signs, whether they be visual or verbal, are clearly narrowed in their activated significatory range through their combination with other signs (Morley 1981 discusses this point usefully).

Whatever the reason for this assumption of general textual 'openness', such a perspective neglects among other things the considerable degree of *determinacy* possessed by texts. This determinacy is simply a result of their using, among other things, systems of signification based on widespread social/national acceptance and having relatively low levels of ambiguity. Terry Eagleton (1983) brings this out very well in dis-cussing aspects of the argument about text–reader relations within literary studies:

You can say that perceiving eleven black marks as the word 'nightingale' is an interpretation, or that perceiving something as black or eleven or a word is an interpretation, and you would be right; but if in most circumstances you read those marks to mean 'nightgown' you would be wrong. An interpretation on which everyone is likely to agree is one way of defining a fact ... Interpreting these marks is a constrained affair, because the marks are often used by people in their social practices of communication in certain ways, and these practical social uses *are* the various meanings of the word. (p. 86)

Eagleton's example could easily be exchanged for one from a newspaper article or from the speech of a television documentary. It is less easy to transfer it across directly to the use of images since the system of image signification (still or moving) is nowhere near as tightly codified as writing and speech, but the basic point about textually-exerted constraints on meaning still obtains. It clearly remains true, as the new interpretative perspective is keen to point out, that 'meaning' does *not* inhere within texts, and is far better seen as a property of interpretative production (and therefore, as potentially 'unstable') even where the most uncomplicated and familiar of routine significations are concerned (e.g. NO ENTRY, 'Hello, David'). But the effect of determinate *signification* upon this production is something which the use of the term 'polysemy' has not always recognised and, at its worst, has dismissed (see Jensen 1990a and Curran and Sparks 1991 on some of the political implications here).

One reason for this is the continued dominance in film and media studies of a literary perspective on meaning. In this perspective, 'meaning' (often seen as synonymous with that completed entity 'the reading') nearly always implies what I have indicated above as 'third-level' activity – the considered attribution of significance, socio-cultural relevance and value – and does so principally in relation to the various 'imaginary' satisfactions to be derived from attending to fictional narratives. Valuable and, indeed, now classic examples here would be the work of Ien Ang on regular viewers of *Dallas* and Janice Radway on the readers of romantic fiction (Ang 1985 and Radway 1984). However, if this usage (meaning equals imaginative response) becomes general then a disastrous degree of slippage around the question of textual openess and closure is almost guaranteed. Over the last decade, lack of adequate differentiation here has trapped a number of reflections upon text-audience relations within a fundamental banality of approach from which not even the most ingenious theoretical elaborations can release them (see the critique in Morris 1988). On occasion, assertions of the fact of 'polysemy' have come dangerously close to precluding any real investigative interest either in the social causes and consequences of interpreting things differently or in the operation of cultural power through the media.

By contrast, I would want to argue that the researching *together* of interpretative action and textual signification is still the most important thing for audience research to focus upon. It is clear that investigations at what I have termed the 'secondary' level of activity, conventionally the 'connotative', must be central to this inquiry. For, with non-fictional forms, this is an important level in the operations whereby both textual mechanisms and readerly frames of reference work to generate thematic understandings and evaluations from specific significatory elements. Attention to differences of interpretation here cuts directly into the practices of cultural reproduction. This level has, of course, been the one at which the most interesting text-analytic work in Cultural Studies has operated – connecting 'outwards' both into specific rules of discursive organisation and also, more ambitiously and speculatively, into the thematics of popular consciousness and the movements and conflicts which are observable therein. As I noted above, reception studies have clearly problematised that diagnostic project, with its confident projections straight into viewers' heads, but some of the questions on the earlier agenda are still worthy of the asking, as I shall suggest in my conclusions.

2 GENRE

Genre is a principal factor in the directing of audience choice and of audience expectations ('shall I watch X?, what might it be like?') and in the organising of the subsets of cultural competences and dispositions appropriate for watching, listening to and reading different kinds of thing. Once again, Morley himself has made some useful connections in a postscript essay on the 'Nationwide' project (Morley 1981) but these were sketchy and have received little if any sustained development (though see Jensen 1986 p. 119 for useful comment). Genre is the second area where I believe increased critical attention is required. For without recognition by the researcher that'television', both as a formal system and as a social process, is constituted from often very different communicative forms and activities, the danger is that an essentialistic tendency will, by default, assert itself. Textual analysis of the media has already suffered from this tendency, particularly so analysis of television, where the range of forms and uses is extremely broad yet closure down to medium unification (e.g. 'television is . . .'; 'television portrays . . .'; television cannot . . .') is common (Ellis 1982 provides an influential example). Though the search for characteristics of television–audience relations in respect of communicational and epistemic properties of the medium itself (see Dahlgren 1988) is well worth pursuing, too urgent an approach to a general theory here is bound to reproduce this essentialism.

The most consequential division across the television genres is the most obvious one and one I have referred to already – that between fictional and non-fictional programming. Although this is not always a clean division in formal systems – certain principles of television 'grammar', for instance, apply to both – the levels of referentiality, modes of address, forms of propositional or more associative, symbolic discourse and the presence or otherwise of television's own representatives (e.g. presenter, host, reporter) serve to mark the two areas out into distinctive communicative realms.

The characteristic properties of text–viewer relations in most non-fiction television are primarily to do with kinds of *knowledge*, usually regulated and framed by direct address speech. This is so even if the programme is devised as an entertainment (for instance, a gardening programme, a popular music review, a sports broadcast).

The characteristic properties of text–viewer relations in fictional television are primarily to do with *imaginative pleasure*, particularly the pleasures of dramatic circumstance and of character. In the last few years, there has been a shift away from news and current affairs as the 'paradigm' form for British and American reception studies and towards popular domestic drama series or 'Soaps', particularly the more successful US series. The result of this emphasis has been an intensive linking of work on reception with questions of realism, pleasure, gender and viewing context. The resulting studies and the closely inter-referenced debate which has followed have been productive, but along with the steady institutionalisation of this particular version of the reception agenda has gone a relative lack of interest in questions of perception, comprehension and understanding. In some discussions of reception processes, journalistic genres have been seen as irredeemably *male* and 'closed' in contrast to the progressive *female* 'openness' of the viewing relations typically obtaining in popular drama (see Fiske 1987). This view is rooted in highly speculative ideas about the gendered character of 'polysemy' in relation both to programme intentions and formats and the typical viewing relations encouraged. One consequence of it seems to have been further to reinforce that division between 'public know-ledge' and 'popular culture' perspectives to which I referred at the start of this essay. It is sometimes implied that journalism's drive towards the facts, towards a truth, is naively and obsessively empiricist, and neglectful of the nature of all public communication as creative play, as necessarily 'invention'. However question-begging such a position is, its connection with aspects of postmodernist commentary has given it a surprising degree of influence in one form or another.

In the first problem area outlined above, around 'meaning', I noted how confusions and complacencies had begun to hinder the develop-ment of audience studies. My argument about genre is that too little attention has been paid to how its specificities affect viewing behaviour (including its degrees of intensity and of concurrent room activity) and that, increasingly often, research and arguments focused on 'soap' series have been put into service as indicative of television-in-general. These separate issues of meaning and of genre are, of course, inter-connected in a number of ways, so that conceptual problems with one may well affect clarity of theorisation in dealing with the other. For instance, as I also noted earlier, to talk of the 'meaning' of a fictional text can be to move straight away to a quite generalised level of response. 'Meaning' here is immediately something to do with imaginative relations – something to do with the cultural satisfactions involved in relating to characters and to dramatic situations. The noting of differences at *this* level may be vulnerably close to the everyday observation that, first of all, different people like different things and, secondly, that people often like the same things for different reasons. If unconnected to a sociological programme of inquiry, research topples backwards into the relativities of 'taste' and any generalised theories of cultural power within which the research may appear to be conducted are, in fact, merely a speculative appendage.

Questions both of meaning and of genre are implicated in the third problem area I have chosen to examine – that of context. For revised notions of what constitutes the operative and researchable 'context' or 'setting' for media audience activity have been among the most important points of reassessment in recent research.

3 CONTEXT

Across a number of different areas of humanities and social science inquiry a shift away from 'formalism' in the analysis of meaning (this being regarded as an exclusive concern with matters of discursive form or 'message structure') has entailed a more direct engagement not only with processes of interpretation but also with contexts and settings. This has occurred in different ways within the disciplines of literary studies, musicology, art history and sociology, to take notable instances, as well as in media and cultural studies. However, perhaps the most intensive theorisation of the issue has occurred in linguistics (see Levinson 1983). The aim has been to analyse meaning (across all 'levels', though as I have pointed out this is not usually made explicit) as socially situated.

Immediately, this broadening out of attention from forms to what are seen as constitutive settings of use poses a problem, though it may not be one immediately addressed by the researcher. Put simply, the problem is this – 'what do you include in context and where does context stop?' Or, put the other way round and more dramatically, 'what *don't* we have to consider?', 'what *doesn't* contribute to the construction of meaning here?'

In the case of television studies, I think it is helpful to see the attempt to 'situate' acts of viewing as an attempt to relate analysis to *two* contextual realms not simply one – the *social relations* of viewing and the *space/time settings* of viewing. These are not usefully conflated and I want to explore a little further what is entailed in researching them in the light of the two basic questions posed above. Investigation into the social relations of viewing carries the reception researcher into the multiple and complex structures and processes which might bear on the *sociality* of interpretative action. Among these are the 'objective' demographic variables – class, gender and age being clearly prominent – but also those less easily plottable yet often highly significant variations in disposition and 'cultural competence' (including familiarity with particular linguistic and aesthetic conventions) which occur *within* as well as between the conventional sociological categorisations. It was part of the conclusion of *The 'Nationwide' Audience* that these latter variables, conceptualised by Morley as the positioning of audience members in varying kinds of 'discursive space', giving a different resourcing to individual practical consciousness, were more significant than his initial hypotheses had suggested. They frequently over-rode or confounded the broad system of socio-economic sampling which had been central to his research design. Further development here has been slow, despite wide discussion of the issues involved (see for instance Brunt and Jordin 1988 for an excellent account of demographic issues in reception surveys). Clearly, classificatory schemes which can work at an intermediate level are necessary, however tentatively projected, if research is not to be caught between unhelpfully broad social typologies on the one hand and banal and unproductive truisms about individual uniqueness on the other. As I shall suggest later, such schemes might involve theme-specific categories (viewer interpretations of economic accounts, for instance, being likely to produce a different pattern of variation from that generated by directly political accounts). They might also explore viewers' occupational variables (types, conditions and experiences of work) more thoroughly and sensitively.

It is in the second, albeit connected realm – that of inquiry into the space/time settings of viewing – that major development has occurred recently. The most ambitious work here at the time of writing is the ongoing project of Morley and Silverstone at Brunel University (see Morley and Silverstone 1990), a project which not only engages with television viewing but with the full range of use of information technology in the home. An emphasis on the situating of viewing in its space and time contexts does not give up on the analysis of general social relations but tries to trace these through the daily routines and rituals of a domestic life within which television may be watched with varying degrees of attention and disattention and concurrently with a number of other household activities and chores (influential earlier studies here were Collett and Lamb 1986 and Morley 1986). Such an emphasis places reception analysis within a 'micro-sociology of every-day life', the better to catch at the constituent moods, motives and rituals of viewing.

One of the problems which seems to follow from working within this perspective is that it then becomes difficult if not impossible to research around single text–viewer relations. Indeed, these become conceptually displaced by the more general relationship obtaining between television and home-life. Moreover, the preferred research methodology itself, in its concern for obtaining situated ethnographic data, tends to be wary of even such limited 'experimental' procedures as the special screening of video material to generate discussion. Thus, insofar as the specific significatory work of television is registered in such research, it is most often at the level of the favourite series or genre of programme. Such information is often richly informative, and it opens television research to perspectives on *use* under-explored within earlier conceptualisations of text–viewer interaction. For instance, it shows *how* in general the flow of meanings from programmes is rhythmically absorbed and made active within daily conversations, the conduct of hobbies and enthusiasms and the organisation of daily life. Nevertheless, localised moments of signification, turning the elements and structures of programmes into sense, are still the nodal points around which the social dynamics of television operate. An under-standing of the scale and subtlety of the 'life-worlds' within which acts of viewing are set must inform but cannot replace attention to these. This is particularly so where the medium's *more direct* public knowledge functions, rather than its breadth of culturally reproductive entertain-ments, are under scrutiny. Displacement here reinforces the displace-ment which I noted earlier in the shift in attention towards fictional genres.

Given the current promise of 'situated' studies, it is also quite easy to *over*-state the extent to which the removal of acts of viewing from the naturalised and fragmented flow of mundane use – such as occurs in the case of researcher-organised screenings – creates an unacceptable degree of distortion in viewers' responses. As well as the relativities of situation, there are the continuities and carry-overs of formed personal identity, preferences and attitudes to take account of here as well as the significatory stabilities of the texts themselves. These are all partial and interdependent constituents of 'meaning-for-the-viewer' but exclusive emphasis on the former within a strong theory of context-dependency risks a situation in which the research forever circles inquisitively around an object which it has, theoretically, abolished. As Charlotte Brunsdon has recently put it:

> The fact that the text is only and always realized in historically and contextually situated practices of reading does not demand that we collapse these categories into each other. (Brunsdon 1989, p. 126)

I suggested earlier that a basic problem presented to all contextually-focused communications research concerns where the 'edges' of relevant context are to be drawn. As well as deciding on an order of significance among all those things which can be designated as 'contextual' in relation to the main object of study (an order which can, of course, be modified in the course of the research), reception analysts also have to decide on those *methods* which will register significant things with appropriate detail and precision. This is by no means a novel situation for social research, but what may be remarkable is the degree to which the significant is not directly accessible to the researcher. For many things which make up the experiential fabric within which situated acts of reading occur are only registerable at all via speculation from data variously and perhaps obliquely held to be indexical of them. The size of this gap between the 'relevant context' and the 'researchable context' may be peculiar to work in the sociology of meanings. The study of attitudes and opinions, for example, though it also works with the unobservable, has conventionally been able to place a good deal of evidential weight (however critically framed) on the recorded statements of respondents *directly* engaging with and articulating the topic under research.

Given the presence of such a gap, there seems to me to be almost a strain of self-destructiveness at work in some of the current enthusiasm for extending contexts of analysis ever broader at the same time as holding out for an increased ethnographic depth. In a recent and generally very perceptive article, even Ien Ang, one of the most prominent and theoretically alert of recent researchers, talked of the need for a 'globalisation' of the ethnographic pursuit' (Ang 1990, p. 244) without registering as much as might be deemed necessary the problems involved in pushing one, albeit sensitive, method of data collection that far out. Peter Dahlgren speculates with equivalent ambition, but with a resoluteness of tone that suggests a stronger sense of the formidable tasks that may lay ahead:

> It may well be that our only methodological option is to seriously launch ourselves on the path of anthropological 'thick descriptions' of the interface of everyday life's many settings with the media environment. (Dahlgren 1988, p. 298).

In its intellectually honourable bid to reject the grand theoreticist generalisations so disabling of media studies in the 1970s, such a project is at risk of being confounded by its own empirical ambition. Just as confusions about meaning and insufficient attention to genre have exerted a limiting effect, so will an under-theorised and imprudently comprehensive notion of the contextual.

VIEWERS-CONSUMERS-CITIZENS: WHERE TO FROM HERE?

Having discussed some of the problems which I believe the new emphasis on interpretation has run into but not always addressed, I want to end positively by indicating very briefly those areas where it seems to me the promise of the new paradigm is considerable. My emphasis here on non-fictional output does not blind me to the great interest and importance of further reception work on TV's dramatic forms, particularly its forms of comedy, which certainly deserve far more attention than has so far been given them. The possibilities I have in mind reject the complacent relativism by which the interpretative contribution of the audience is perceived to be of such a scale and range as to render the very idea of media power naive. They also reject a rather different, if equally influential view – the radical populist presumption that popular audiences can be trusted to exercise an almost instinctive capacity to 'resist'[3] most of what they attend to via the media, apparently through mechanisms of cognition, thought process and overall social motivation not thought to require any further, closer attention.

These possibilities offer the chance to connect ideas of interpretative variation and its social determinants with the continuing debate about the media's function in organising and disseminating public knowledge. They therefore engage with the 'influence' agenda. However much that agenda has had to be modified since the (mythical?) period when it was researched in terms of direct, monocausal processes of mental or behavioural change, the consequences of media systems for the consciousness and actions of the audience/public remain the most important goal of media inquiry. In a recent overview of research in Western Europe, Jay Blumler *et al.* called for more attention to 'citizen-readers' and for inquiry into:

> questions about how major political institutions and processes, including their symbolic meanings or claims, are 'read' and interpreted by those who follow reports about them in the mass media. (Blumler *et al.* 1990, pp. 275–6)

Peter Golding has also made a claim for 'the resurrection of the concept of citizenship as a critical bench-mark of enquiry in communications research' (Golding 1990, p. 100). To a degree, such an essentially public concept might act as a corrective complement to the rhetoric of the privatised 'consumer', which has undergone such opportunistic expansion in recent policy debate and which has sometimes achieved an odd and facile alignment with research emphases on 'pleasure'. How might a re-focused reception studies converge with the kind of enquiry looked for by Golding?

First of all, I think, by attempting to connect back to some quite old questions about the 'everyday' forms of comprehension of the social and political realm which are variously constitutive of civic disposition and opinion. How *is* public knowledge around particular nodal themes like 'the economy', 'defence', 'energy', 'health' and 'education' actually resourced from the variety of images, concepts, explanations and testimonies differentially available through media channels, as one set of agencies among others but ones central to the interconnecting of private and public realms?

Address to this question will require the interconnecting of cultural studies and sociological perspectives with those of social psychology and linguistics. The to and fro movements which I referred to earlier, between the different levels of activity constitutive of 'making sense', will only yield to analysis of such an interdisciplinary kind. So the sort of project I am outlining, though it can certainly find some guidance from previous attempts to plot and theorise 'attitudes and opinions', is distinctive in its address both to the detail of communicative form *and* to those factors of interpretative activity which recent work on reception has so indelibly placed on the research agenda. To turn to the conceptual apparatus which such research could employ, patterns of variation in the distribution, uptake and use of 'public knowledge' might productively be addressed by applying a range of interest group, occupational and political affiliation categories in addition to the main socio-demographic factors. Jensen (1990a) indicates how the modes of viewing of informational television might be differentiated in relation to use-values and, in an innovative attempt at bridging empirical research foci, in relation to the actual patterns of channel selection (1990b). Dahlgren (1988) has offered an account of how TV-initiated talk about public affairs can, itself, be generically defined.

Projects primarily designed not by reference to specific groups, settings or genres but to specific public issues receiving media treatment within different generic conventions could be particularly illuminating. A splendid example, which stopped short of a reception study, is Schlesinger, Murdock and Elliott (1983) on 'terrorism'. By holding the topic and its constituent themes constant, a sharper address to multi-levelled (including visual) meaning can be achieved whilst at the same time the edges of researchable, relevant context can be more explicitly addressed. The goal here lies well beyond some further demonstrating of 'variation' among the 'active audience'. It lies in the closest possible engagement with the resources, terms and (to use a Stuart Hall phrase) the 'logics-in-use' out of which the forms of public, practical consciousness are made. Philo (1990) on public perceptions of the terms of the news coverage around the British Coal Strike and Corner, Richardson and Fenton (1990a and 1990b) on responses to TV depictions of Nuclear Energy policy have recently shown some of the possibilities. More importantly, they have also shown that close attention to 'interpretation' can, far from displacing the idea of 'influence', bring research on the formation of public and political knowledge back to it with sharper focus and renewed theoretical confidence.

NOTES

1. I believe that reception research can profit from an understanding of how the debate between 'semantic' and 'pragmatic' perspectives has developed in linguistics. This debate, sometimes conducted from positions close to mutual exclusion, has not only encouraged close attention to the significatory factors involved in the production of meaning, it has brought analysis to bear on the idea of 'relevant context' and the problems of researching this. See Levinson (1983) for an excellent and lively discussion.

2. Hjelmslev (1953) offers some detailed discussion of this distinction at a date prior to its being taken up within cultural analysis through the various writings of Barthes and Eco. Eco (1976) is one of the clearest accounts I have come across though it is certainly not without its problems. It contains this interesting comment:

> The difference between denotation and connotation is not (as many authors maintain) the difference between 'univocal' and 'vague' signification, or between 'referential' and 'emotional' communication, and so on. What constitutes a connotation as such is the connotative code which establishes it; the characteristic of a connotative code is the fact that the further signification conventionally relies on a primary one . . . (pp. 55–6)

Clearly, this idea of a stage of 'higher' signification being built upon the codes of lower ones is behind Barthes' hugely influential, 'three-decker' theory of myth (Barthes 1972). I am using a three-level schema less grandly and less evaluatively, as a way into differentiating more finely the processes of mundane meaning-making.

3. It is perhaps worth noting how ideas of the 'resisting' viewer are frequently linked to theories of 'polysemy', when logic would suggest quite the reverse. A viewer interpreting 'resistively' is consciously working *against* a set of meanings and values which they have (a) attributed to a programme item and (b) assumed to have been intended by the programme makers. Unless one advances a theory in which viewers 'resist' in a variety of different directions with no significant pattern of convergence, this seems to be more an argument for the (social) determinateness of texts than one for their polysemic character.

REFERENCES

Ang, I., 1985: *Watching 'Dallas': Soap opera and the melodramatic imagination.* New York: Methuen.

Ang, I., 1990: 'Culture and Communication: Towards an Ethnographic Critique of Media Consumption in the Transnational Media System' in *European Journal of Communication* 5, 2–3, pp. 239–60.

Barthes, R., 1972: *Mythologies* (trans. A. Lavers). London: Jonathan Cape.

Blumler, J. G., Dayan, D. and Wolton, D., 1990:'West European Perspectives on Political Communication: Structures and Dynamics' in *European Journal of Communication*, 5, 2–3, pp. 261–84.

Bradac, J. (ed.), 1989: *Message effects in communication science*. London: Sage.

Brunsdon, C., 1989: 'Text and Audience' in Ellen Seiter *et al.* (eds) *Remote control: Television, audiences and cultural power*. London: Routledge, pp. 116–29.

Brunt, R. and Jordin, M., 1988:'Constituting the Television Audience: A Problem of Method' in P. Drummond and R. Paterson (eds) *Television and its audience*. London: B.F.I. pp. 231–49.

Collett, P. and Lamb, R., 1986: *Watching families watching TV*. Report to Independent Broadcasting Authority, London.

Corner, J., 1985:'Criticism as Sociology: Reading the Media' in J. Hawthorn (ed.) *Criticism and critical theory*. London: Edward Arnold, pp. 29–41.

Corner, J., Richardson, K. and Fenton, N., 1990a: Textualizing Risk: TV Discourse and the Issue of Nuclear Energy' in *Media, Culture and Society* 12, 1, pp. 105–24.

Corner, J., Richardson, K. and Fenton, N., 1990b: *Nuclear reactions: Form and response in 'public issue' television*. London: John Libbey.

Curran, J., 1990: 'The New Revisionism in Mass Communication Research: A Reappraisal' in *European Journal of Communication* 5, 2–3, pp. 135–64.

Curran, J. and Sparks, C., 1991:'Press and Popular Culture'in *Media, Culture and Society*, 13.2, pp. 215–37.

Dahlgren, P., 1988: 'What's the Meaning of This?: Viewers' Plural Sense-Making of TV News' in *Media, Culture and Society* 10, 3, pp. 285–301.

Eagleton, T., 1983: *Literary theory*. Oxford: Blackwell.

Eco, V., 1976: *A theory of semiotics*. London: Macmillan.

Ellis, J., 1982: *Visible fictions*. London: Routledge.

Fiske, J., 1987: *Television culture*. London: Methuen.

Golding, P., 1990:'Political Communication and Citizenship: The Media and Democracy in an Inegalitarian Social Order' in M. Ferguson (ed.) *Public communication: The new imperative*. London: Sage.

Gripsrud, J., 1989:'"High Culture"Revisited'in *Cultural Studies* 3, 2, pp. 194–207.

Hall, S., 1977:'Culture, the Media and the"Ideological Effect"' in J. Curran, M. Gurevitch and J. Woollacott (eds) *Mass communication and society*. London: Edward Arnold.

Harvey, D., 1989: *The condition of postmodernity*. Oxford: Blackwell.

Hjelmslev, L., 1953: 'Prolegomena to a Theory of Language', Memoir 7 to *International Journal of American Linguistics*. Baltimore: Waverly Press, pp. 1–92.

Hoijer, B., 1990: 'Studying Viewers' Reception of Television Programmes: Theoretical and Methodological Considerations' in *European Journal of Communication* 5,1, pp. 29–56.

Jensen, K., 1986: *Making sense of the news*. Aarhus: The University Press.

Jensen, K., 1990a: 'The Politics of Polysemy: Television News, Everyday Consciousness and Political Action' in *Media, Culture and Society* 12, 1, pp. 57–77.

Jensen, K., 1990b: 'Reception as Flow: The"New Television Viewer"Revisited'. Paper to 17th Conference of the IAMCR, Bled, Jugoslavia, August 1990.

Jensen, K. and Rosengren, E., 1990: 'Five Traditions in Search of the Audience' in *European Journal of Communication* 5, 2–3, pp. 207–38.

Levinson, S., 1983: *Pragmatics*. Cambridge: CUP.

Lewis, J., 1983: 'The Encoding-Decoding Model: Criticisms and Redevelopments for Research on Decoding' in *Media, Culture and Society* 5, 2, pp. 179–97.

Lewis, J., 1985: 'Decoding Television News' in P. Drummond and R. Paterson (eds) *Television in transition*. London: BFI.

Liebes, T. and Katz, E., 1990: *The export of meaning*. Oxford: OUP.

Livingstone, S. M., 1988: 'Viewers' Interpretations of Soap Opera: The Role of Gender, Power and Morality' in P. Drummond and R. Paterson *Television and its audience*. London: BFI.

Moores, S., 1990: 'Texts, Readers and Contexts of Reading: Developments in the Study of Media Audiences' in *Media, Culture and Society* 12, 1, pp. 9–29.

Morley, D, 1980: *The 'Nationwide' audience: structure and decoding*. London: BFI.

Morley, D., 1981: 'The Nationwide Audience: A Critical Postscript' in *Screen Education* 39, pp. 3–14.

Morley, D., 1986: *Family Television*. London: Comedia.

Morley, D., 1989: 'Changing Paradigms in Audience Studies' in E. Seiter *et al.* (eds) *Remote control: Television, audiences and cultural power*. London: Routledge.

Morley, D. and Silverstone, R., 1990: 'Domestic Communication – Technologies and Meanings' in *Media, Culture and Society* 12, 1, pp. 31–55.

Morris, M., 1988: 'Banality in Cultural Studies' in *Block* 14, pp. 15–26.

Philo, G., 1990: *Seeing and believing*. London: Routledge.

Radway, J., 1984: *Reading the romance. Women, patriarchy and popular literature*. Chapel Hill: University of North Carolina Press.

Richardson, K. and Corner, J., 1986: 'Reading Reception: Mediation and Transparency in Viewers' Accounts of a TV Programme' in *Media, Culture and Society* 8, 4, pp. 485–508.

Schlesinger, P., Murdock, G. and Elliott, P., 1983: *Televising 'terrorism': Political violence in popular culture*. London: Comedia.

Schroder, K., 1987: 'Convergence of Antagonistic Traditions? The Case of Audience Research' in *European Journal of Communication* 2, 1, pp. 7–31.

Seiter, E., Borchers, H. Kreutzner, G. and Warth, E.-M., 1989: 'Don't Treat Us
    Like We're So Stupid and Naive': Towards an Ethnography of Soap Opera
    Viewers' in E. Seiter *et al.* (eds) *Remote Control*. London: Routledge, pp.
    223–44.

Chapter 8

DEBATING CULTURE
Quality and Inequality

———⊂⇒———

I attempt here a modest intervention in the broad and long-running debate about cultural tastes and cultural differences, particularly insofar as these have to do with the 'popular'. I wanted to indicate my dissatisfaction with the way in which questions of 'quality' had simply been avoided by much recent cultural research, with relativism establishing itself by a mixture of default and intention. However, there were some signs, for instance Charlotte Brunsdon's cited essay in Screen, that this avoidance of evaluation was now being seen as a failing. One of the consequences of the failing was the continuation of a gap between work in media and cultural analysis and the sphere of media and cultural policy-making, a sphere in which questions of 'standards' and 'quality' were seen to be central if also often controversial.

I focused on the seminal work of Williams and Bourdieu in order to bring out what seemed to me to be moments of unresolved awkwardness in their views about how issues of cultural value relate to issues of cultural stratification and, indeed, perhaps deprivation. The much commented upon duality of the term 'culture' – having both a normative meaning as 'arts/learning' and also a more descriptive, broader meaning as 'ways of life' seemed to lie behind some of the difficulties here.

In a perceptive and cogent essay of response, Paul Jones ('Williams and "Quality"', Media, Culture and Society 17.2. 1995, 317–22) accused me of selecting so narrowly from Williams's writings as to distort the real attempt he had made to argue for a new, democratic

135

*way of thinking about culture that overcame some of the difficulties
which my article identified. I accept the charge of polemical foreshortening, but I still regard the Williams essay from which I cite as
indicative of a problem, both for him and, continuingly, for others.
More recently, John Frow's Cultural Studies and Cultural Value (Oxford:
Clarendon Press, 1995) provides an impressive account of 'economies
of value', with some suggestions as to how academics might better
engage with cultural judgement and cultural hierarchies.*

Questions about 'quality' have been raised in a number of recent
commentaries on cultural theory and cultural policy. Brunsdon (1990)
sought to re-engage debate about aesthetic criteria in television research
while the essays collected in Mulgan (1990) addressed television quality
as a key term in what was then the intensifying British debate about
the funding and regulation of broadcasting. With colleagues, I have
recently reviewed the use of 'quality' criteria in that debate, focusing on
one of its major legislative outcomes, the ITV franchise allocations of
1991 (Corner et al., 1993). Schroder (1992) examines the notion critically
in relation to research on audiences for popular television, and the
growing body of commentary on the 'problem of populism' in cultural
analysis also carries implications for questions of cultural value (as
Frith, 1991, and McGuigan, 1992, bring out clearly).

In this note I want to explore some problems with conceptualising
cultural quality and to trace its connections with the idea of cultural
*in*equality. I shall argue that the relationship is much stronger than
suggestive wordplay; that, indeed, the two terms constitute an interdefining couplet, though they are not often explicitly recognised as
paired. This couplet, linking aesthetic to social evaluation, continues to
be a central one in thinking through the whole question of power
relations in culture and it continues to be an extremely awkward one
to handle with clarity and consistency. I shall try to open up some
aspects of this awkwardness by reference to the perspectives on 'quality' of Raymond Williams and Pierre Bourdieu.

Before looking at their work, however, it might be useful to examine
the basic terms of what I have suggested is the quality/inequality
couplet.

Issues of 'cultural quality' turn on the criteria by which judgements about cultural artefacts and related processes and experiences can be made. The question is essentially 'What is good?' and it is quite clearly a question with a distinguished classical lineage. The principal terms are directly aesthetic and ethical in character, whatever their wider socio-political constitution.

In cultural debate, the *inequality* issue turns essentially on there not being a 'fair' distribution of good things. So whereas 'quality' is primarily a judgement of artefacts (however much reification is recognised as a risk), 'inequality' is a judgement of relative social circumstances and conditions. The 'unfairness' can be seen as a straight matter of distribution (e.g. who can and who cannot afford satellite television, or who has an art gallery, a concert hall or a library within accessible distance) or, in a more complex and indirect way, as a matter, too, of the unequal distribution of the cultural dispositions and competences by which cultural goodness can be accessed, appreciated and 'used'.

Inequality cannot be argued for without some criteria concerning the particular goodness (quality) which is being unequally distributed. These will ground the argument as to why precisely it is *bad* that some people are not in receipt of it. Likewise, all systems of qualitative judgement necessarily involve some idea of inequality insofar as there will be those things which, when assessed in relation to the system's standards, are judged as *not* good. Those people who (for whatever reason) choose the culturally 'not good' may have their personal affective order ('sensibility') and indeed their general consciousness rendered suspect in the eyes of others as a result of this judgement.[1] Such suspicion, depending on the form of its articulation with other views, might confirm conservative social prejudice or provide further evidence of the need for radical change.

An illuminating instance of just this kind of quality/inequality configuration is to be found in an important, early essay by Williams, 'Culture is Ordinary' (1989, orig. 1958). The essay was written against what was perceived by the author as a dominant, literary-based elitism within whose terms the 'culture' of ordinary people was either ignored or actively dis-valued. It is important to remember that part of Williams's terms of response here involved a usage of the term 'culture' broadened out from one exclusively based on an 'arts and learning' definition to one which connected with what is now most often referred to as the 'anthropological' definition – culture as a 'whole way of life'. Within the broad definition, however, the narrow one remains active as a core, giving the new usage a duality and even ambiguity. Williams employs this to good polemical effect but, as I shall argue later, it runs the risk of collapsing art and society together into an uncertain *unity* when it is precisely the relationship between the two which requires analysis.

Having identified and rejected a 'first false equation' in contemporary British cultural debate, an equation which would place the commercial culture of the late Industrial Revolution as an inevitable consequence of popular education, Williams moves on to engage with a 'second false equation':

> The second false equation is this: that the observable badness of so much widely distributed popular culture is a true guide to the state of mind and feeling, the essential quality of living of its consumers. . . . It is easy to assemble, from print and cinema and television, a terrifying and fantastic congress of cheap feelings and moronic arguments. It is easy to go on from this and assume this deeply degrading version of the actual lives of our contemporaries. Yet do we find this confirmed when we meet people? This is where 'masses' comes in again, of course: the people we meet aren't vulgar. . . . A few weeks ago I was in a house with a commercial traveller, a lorry driver, a bricklayer, a shopgirl, a fitter, a signalman, a nylon operative, a domestic help. . . . I hate describing people like this, for in fact they were my family and family friends. Now they read, they watch, this work we are talking about, some of them quite critically, others with a good deal of pleasure. Very well, I read different things, watch different entertainments, *and I am quite sure why they are better*. But could I sit down in that house and make this equation we are offered? . . . *could I in fact find this lack of quality we are discussing?* I'll be honest – I looked; my training has done that for me. I can only say that I found as much natural fineness of feeling, as much quick discrimination, as much clear grasp of ideas within the range of experience as I have found anywhere. I don't altogether understand this, though I am not really surprised. (Williams, 1989: 12–13; emphases added)

In this passage, a number of tensions are discernible. The discriminating, evaluative skills of the academy ('my training') apparently receive personal authentication from Williams, along with the broad system of values they conventionally underpin (he does not question or problematise the 'observable badness'). But they are in implicit conflict with his experiential (and here familial) assessment of 'ordinary people'. According to the expanded literary culturalism informing his account, 'bad texts' should imply both a degree of 'bad sensibility' and a consequent degree of 'badness' in life quality. Such a culturalism presumes a relatively direct inter-linkage between culture (expressive artefacts) and culture (way of life). Williams's own experiential data falsifies the neatness of the interconnection and he recognises this. What he fails to recognise is that the falsification then leaves him without any clear way of arguing for the existence of cultural inequality or deprivation, for anything that needs *redress*. For if people do not appear impaired by their exposure to the presently 'popular', on what grounds can the claim of inequality be sustained? In an argument advocating radical reform of the media, uncertainty here presents a major snag. I don't want to suggest that breaking out from the contradiction is easy – it is a contradiction indicative of broader and continuing tensions between the 'elitist' and 'populist' dynamics of British cultural analysis. However, a more reflexive and explicit theory of cultural reproduction and a more differentiated sense of the informational as against the entertainment functions and consequences of the 'popular' would provide a useful start.

I want to turn now to Bourdieu, in order to see how my two key notions relate in his very different conceptual universe. Bourdieu's perspective on culture is clearly that of a sociologist of taste, and in his major work, *Distinction* (1984), tastes are viewed primarily as kinds of positional goods (as manifestations of cultural capital) within the cultural economy. 'Quality' is therefore seen as a rationalisation of positional power; an attribution of value (or of disvalue) normally made from within the dominant class framework of evaluation.

However, although Bourdieu's account of culture-as-system implies a depersonalised, objective mode of study (one which therefore contrasts strongly with the mode characteristically used by Williams), and although it is supported by an impressive density of sociologically-assembled data, there is a strand of evaluation at work in it which at times bears more directly on the propositional structure of the piece than does the 'scientific' framework.[2] Self-declared as a reflexive researcher, Bourdieu does not reflect much if at all on the criteria used in this evaluation, or on the implications it might hold for his own class position as a person of tastes. The vulnerability of the procedure is partly hidden by the fact that Bourdieu's considerable evaluative wit is applied, if often covertly, to *both* sides of that taste polarity – the pure against the popular – which is a central feature of his scheme. Here he is on some of the defining characteristics of popular taste:

> The hostility of the working class and of the middle-class fractions less rich in cultural capital towards every kind of formal experimen-tation asserts itself both in the theatre and in painting, or, still more clearly because they have less legitimacy, in photography and the cinema. In the theatre as in the cinema, the popular audience delights in plots that proceed logically and chronologi-cally towards a happy end, and 'identifies' better with simply drawn situations and characters than with ambiguous and symbolic figures and actions . . . (Bourdieu, 1984: 31)

Despite the descriptive coolness here, it is hard to read the 'hostility' which Bourdieu attributes to popular taste as other than naive in its origin, a simplicity of taste based on a simplicity of mind, as it were. The relative sophistication of Bourdieu's own tastes (e.g. the capacity to handle complex aesthetic form) gives a 'stance' to his account, one not entirely escaping condescension, which is neither reflexively monitored nor acknowledged.

A more explicit judgement is at work in his much-quoted account of the contrasting cultural disposition – that of the 'pure gaze':

> The pure gaze implies a break with the ordinary attitude towards the world which, as such, is a social break . . . [This] clearly means rejecting what is generic, i.e. *common*, 'easy', and immediately accessible, starting with everything that reduces the aesthetic animal to pure and simple animality, to palpable pleasure or sensual desire. The interest in the content of the representation which leads people to call 'beautiful' the representation of beautiful things . . . is rejected in favour of the indifference and distance

which refuse to subordinate judgement of the representation to the nature of the object represented. (Bourdieu, 1984: 31–2)

In his discussion of Popular Taste, Bourdieu implies, I believe, that such 'subordination' is partly grounded in naivety. Here, within the realm of Refined Taste, the *rejection* of this subordination is seen as a distortion of common humanity. Although his accounts of both tastes contain passages of polemical exaggeration and wry distancing (as carried, for instance, in the phrase 'pure and simple animality'), criteria are not as clear as they might be.[3]

We can nevertheless plot Bourdieu's position as one lying some-where between two broad and unsatisfactory 'taste dispositions', the one unsatisfactorily naive, the other unsatisfactorily refined. It is a position which, as I have suggested, is neither socialised by reference to a specific class or professional sub-group nor personalised by ref-erence to his own cultural choices.

While in the case of Williams we have a cultural theorist attempting to engage with a quality/inequality tension the precise dimensions and contradictions of which he is unable fully to address or monitor, in Bourdieu we have a cultural theorist whose confident terms of analysis register no tension whatsoever but whose entire argument is indicative of fundamental evaluative ambiguity.

Nor can this be regarded as a secondary matter of 'slippage' from description into evaluation, since, as with Williams, the whole question of cultural value is implicated in the kind of 'inequality' which Bourdieu wishes to demonstrate and in the kind of policy, radical or reformist, which would work to bring about a degree of *equalisation*.

The big question posed by Bourdieu's terms of analysis is this – is the real problem for him the unequal social distribution of cultural dispositions and competences? Or is it the power of those with cultural capital to impose a system of cultural value which fits in with their own tastes? Put another way, does Bourdieu hold to certain cultural *values* (necessarily, we can agree, contingent rather than transcendent), the social accessibility and appreciation of which have been distorted by economic and educational inequalities? Or is he a relativist, bent on deconstructing a dominant, class-based absolutism? The implications of the answer for *any* sense of 'What is to be done?' in terms of national cultural and educational policy are crucial.

It is my contention that Cultural Studies has found it very hard not to reproduce versions of the two kinds of ambivalence or ambiguity illustrated above within the varied theoretical and empirical work done over the last decade. In fact, the difficulties which I have documented have been joined by other more recent factors to put the conceptualisation of quality and inequality into near crisis. Among these factors I would note three in particular. First of all, the widespread if multifarious influence of postmodernist thinking, with its strong emphasis on cultural relativism, diversity and difference and its tendency either to avoid, infinitely postpone or diminish questions of cultural power. Second, the rise of ethnographic enquiry in media and popular cultural studies. The 'bottom up' accounts produced here too often (and, I think, increasingly) get trapped in a kind of *populist descriptivism*, in which detailed documentation of popular experience takes on an affirmatory self-sufficiency unrelated to any general political or social theory.[4] Finally, there is the increased tendency to place the arts, education and media more firmly within a framework of market relations. With considerable national variation, this has promoted the idea of 'market democracy', a political order based on consumer power and committed to relativising taste in relation to consumer demand (implicitly classifying all objections to this as 'elitist'). This tendency has worked to displace the essentially critical notion of cultural inequality and to substitute the potentially complacent notions of cultural 'difference' and of cultural 'choice'. A number of postmodern cultural commentators have aligned themselves behind this shift (regarding it as 'tomorrow's reality' with varying degrees of regret or enthusiasm), thereby giving it accommodation within the new high theory.

I want to conclude by suggesting some lines of investigation which might serve to open up for more thorough debate the principal issues which I have tried to raise.

First, cultural analysis needs to engage far more closely with questions about the relationship between 'the arts', self-development and subjectivity. This is a whole area of human social experience, of lived values and of emancipatory energies, which has not figured significantly in recent analysis. It is an area which cuts across the duality of the concept of culture. It raises questions not only about the specific character of the various art forms but about the social relations of the categories of the 'serious' and the 'entertaining' as they figure locally, in everyday life, as well as in a national cultural order. Questions are posed, too, about the *intellectual* dimension of expressive activity, questions which have too often suffered from polemical foreshortening within the terms of the elitist/populist debate. Attention to the psychodynamics of aesthetic response needs to figure strongly in this enquiry, though they warrant a more defined articulation with the political, the social and the historical than has often been the case in literary and cinema studies. The interplay of use-value and exchange value in aesthetic evaluation, the particular gratificatory economies within which differentiations are made and produced pleasures validated (or perhaps enjoyed as 'outlawed') requires an attention which is able to think subjectivity *sociologically*.

Second, Cultural Studies should retain its founding emphasis on the socially differentiated and political character of cultural experience and on the contingency of aesthetic practice,[5] but it should support those policies (some of which are traditionally liberal) seeking to provide all people with the widest possible access to, and means to enjoy, conventionally 'high' aesthetic forms. The rejection of these as irredeemably middle-class is, like the wholesale dismissal of 'popular culture' by elite commentators, a prescriptive narrowing of cultural experience derived from false socio-political assumptions.

Third, following on from my first point, more investigation into the clusterings of taste-choices and evaluation (of popular *discrimination*) across different cultural forms is necessary. Just *how* differentiated access, dispositions, competences and judgements come about in contemporary society through a mix of economic, social and personal factors should be a question on a variety of research agendas (see Laermans, 1992, for suggestions about researching evaluative hierarchies and Clifford, 1988, for an anthropological approach to art-culture classifications). This is to press well beyond the minimalist indications of Bourdieu's questionnaire responses, however irreplaceable his work remains as a broad precedent. At the moment, there is too much speculation, and too little data, on how people organise their lives within the range of cultural options and taste configurations ('either/or' as well as 'both/and') available to them.[6]

Finally, what also needs to be addressed is the strong indication that the very notion of 'culture' has become a block to clear thinking about the interpenetration of aesthetic practices and social processes and structures. Its accommodating softness as a concept, its unmonitored movements of focus across the art/society dualism, have too often made it of service to a lazy, totalising assertiveness which has blurred issues and ignored differentiation. In thinking through the interdefining tensions of quality and inequality in contemporary arts, media and entertainment, some deconstructive pressure on the concept of 'culture' would be no bad thing.

NOTES

An earlier version of this article was presented and circulated as a paper to the conference of the Association for Media, Film and Television Studies, University of London, March 1992. I am grateful for the comments made on this draft by Sylvia Harvey.

1. Although I go on to identify a problem with the application of ideas about quality in Raymond Williams's media criticism, he shows himself to be well aware of this kind of slippage. For instance:

    The utmost emphasis on distinctions of value . . . is not an empha-
    sis on inequality of being. It is, rather, a common process of learning,
    which, indeed, will only ever be undertaken if the primary conces-
    sion of equality of being, which alone can remove such a process
    from the dominative sphere, is made. Nobody can raise anybody
    else's cultural standards. (Williams, 1958: 318)

    In his early work, however, Williams was inclined to underestimate the economic and social obstacles to achieving even the minimum conditions for a 'common process of learning'. In this sense, his comments have a disabling (because deceptive) utopian aspect, though not, I think, on such a scale as to invalidate them.
2. Some fundamental problems with Bourdieu's whole methodology here, as well as with his theories, are well brought out in John Frow (1987). The difference between Bourdieu's positionalist view of the 'cultural system' and the expressive/affective, though still structural, commentary of Raymond Williams is assessed in Mander (1987). LiPuma (1993) notes how Bourdieu's functionalist view of 'distinction' requires a degree of arbitrariness in cultural products which effectively makes meaning a residual category. A reductive aesthetics is not the only consequence of this; it has implications for the explanatory force of Bourdieu's account of cultural reproduction at the level of individualised affect and cogni-tion. For instance, it sometimes appears from this account that those working from within the 'refined' aesthetic disposition are engaged in a

sustained and strategic game of cultural bluff. Yet the social psychology of this (implausible) state of affairs, in terms of the lived experience of desire and fulfilment, does not receive the attention which it then deserves.

3. A rather different interpretation of these pages in *Distinction*, taking the view that Bourdieu consistently affirms the popular aesthetic, is to be found in Schroder (1992). Schroder's own argument is grounded in audience studies and it warns against the anti-democratic consequences of attempting any 'return to "quality"' in academic work on television. Despite the cogency with which the case is argued, I judge Schroder's final position to be more relativist than I am prepared to accept. However, his brief and thoughtful discussion of Bourdieu confirms my sense of the ambiguity and perhaps ambivalence to be found in the key passages.

4. A comprehensive though occasionally 'potted' discussion of populist tendencies in cultural studies is given in McGuigan (1992). The current dangers of populism in popular arts criticism are usefully reviewed in Frith (1991).

5. Smith (1988) offers a vigorously argued and often entertaining account of the contingency of normative aesthetic judgement, including the various 'objectivist' moves used to suppress this contingency and to underpin such ideas as 'taste development'. In my view, her demolition work does not undercut the possibility of arguing 'cultural quality' in the public sphere, though it certainly highlights the hazards of doing so. On questions of absolutism and relativism in aesthetic theory and the 'paradox of value', see also the perceptive commentary in Connor (1992).

6. Paul Willis et al. (1990) discuss contemporary cultural choice and pleasure in the context of a wide-ranging youth ethnography. However, despite its strength of approach and data, it ends up with a very dispersed and sometimes evasive notion of aesthetics. Its generally upbeat conclusions can be contrasted with those of Lee (1993), who examines the distinctive forms of commodified sensibility which recent shifts in patterns and modes of consumption have encouraged.

REFERENCES

Bourdieu, P. (1984) *Distinction*, trans. Richard Nice. London: Routledge.

Brunsdon, C. (1990) 'Quality in Television', *Screen*, 31(1): 67–90.

Clifford, J. (1988) *The Predicament of Culture*. Cambridge, MA and London: Harvard University Press.

Connor, S. (1992) *Theory and Cultural Value*. Oxford: Blackwell.

Corner, J., S. Harvey and K. Lury (1993) 'British Television and the "Quality" Issue', *Media Information Australia*, 68: 78–85.

Frith, S. (1991) 'The Good, the Bad and the Indifferent: Defending Popular Culture From the Populists', *Diacritics*, 21(Winter): 102–15.

Frow, J. (1987) 'Accounting for Taste: Some Problems in Bourdieu's Sociology of Culture', *Cultural Studies*, 1(1): 59–73.

Laermans, R. (1992) 'The Relative Rightness of Pierre Bourdieu', *Cultural Studies*, 6(2): 248–59.

Lee, M. (1993) *Consumer Culture Reborn: The Cultural Politics of Consumption*. London: Routledge.

LiPuma, E. (1993) 'Culture and the Concept of Culture in a Theory of Practice', pp. 14–34 C. Calhoun, et al. (eds), *Bourdieu: Critical Perspectives*. Cambridge: Polity Press.

McGuigan, J. (1992) *Cultural Populism*. London: Routledge.

Mander, M. (1987) 'Bourdieu, the Sociology of Culture and Cultural Studies', *European Journal of Communication*, 2(1): 427–53.

Mulgan, G. (ed.) (1990) *The Question of Quality*. London: British Film Institute.

Schroder, K. (1992) 'Cultural Quality: Search for a Phantom?' pp. 199–219 in M. Skovmand and K. Schroder (eds), *Media Cultures*. London: Routledge.

Smith, B. H. (1988) *Contingencies of Value*. Cambridge, MA: Harvard University Press.

Willis, P., S. Jones, J. Canaan and G. Hurd (1990) *Common Culture*. Milton Keynes: Open University Press.

Williams, R. (1958) *Culture and Society 1780–1950*. London: Chatto and Windus.

Williams, R. (1989) 'Culture is Ordinary', pp. 3–18 in *Resources of Hope*. London: Verso. First published 1958.

Chapter 9

TELEVISION IN THEORY

———— ⊃⊂ ————

I offer here a critical audit of theoretical work on television, looking at this under four classifications. I also try to raise more general questions, referred to in the introduction to this book, about the status of theory and its relationship to analysis and data in media research. We can benefit from recent reflections about the nature of the 'theoretical' to be found elsewhere in the social sciences and in the natural sciences too. Perhaps it is worth saying that this is not an 'anti-theoretical' polemic, whatever that would look like as an academic exercise. It sees theorising as an essential activity of inquiry but identifies problems both with the present status and character of 'theory' and the quality of some theories dominant within the field.

Television has attracted much theoretical attention over the last two decades. Work from a number of different perspectives has attempted to locate different aspects of television within conceptual schemes which might help to explain its nature, operation and consequences. The sheer scale of its depictive 'flows' within modern society and its character as a representational matrix installed at the intersection of public and private life, have been an inviting challenge for such work. Some approaches to general social and cultural theory have located television in their broader schemes, often giving it a significance not found in earlier accounts. But there has also been a good deal of television-centred work undertaken, especially within the interdisciplinary framework of 'media studies'. Some of this work has been television-centred in its substantive interests while drawing on a wide range of theoretical and empirical settings in which to place the medium. Some of it has had a more exclusive character, developing its theoretical project tightly around television with little by way of cross-connection with existing social theory and research. Not surprisingly, work on tele-vision as an industry has shown less exclusivity than work on television texts, with recent work on audiences varying considerably in the kinds of conceptual linkage to the non-televisual which it attempts to make.

Compared to most areas of social science, most work on television has shown less by way of *theory building* and *theory development* in relation to research and analysis. And although there has been a degree of interperspectival debate, theoretical developments have often occurred in relative isolation from each other. Notwithstanding the continuing value of many ideas and concepts, an over-privileged and under-accountable role for theory and for the 'theorist' has become established.

Here, I want to attempt a brief critical audit of theoretical approaches to television, looking at some of the limitations which have shown themselves and at directions for the future. First of all, it would be use-ful to examine what is indicated by describing certain kinds of enquiry as 'theoretical', or by calling a particular set of ideas about television a 'theory', since the literature of international media research displays shifts and uncertainties of usage.

THEORY AS AN ACADEMIC PRACTICE

In his recent general account of cultural theory (Fornäs, 1995), Johan Fornäs reminds us that the Greek roots of 'theory' lie in the idea of see-ing or beholding (a point not without some irony given the problems of obscurity from which media studies has suffered). More generally, 'theory' locates phenomena within a context of explicatory abstraction, seeking to understand them at a level above that of descriptive detail, a level where their interconnection with other phenomena and their generalised significance within the 'systems' constituted by perceived laws and conventions and bodies of previous knowledge can be gauged. Theories vary in their scale and internal complexity, ranging from a single speculative idea to linked series of propositions and conceptual *systems* claiming a degree of predictive precision. In the natural sciences, developed theoretical constructs are often produced partly from the empirical testing of hypotheses (although these are themselves variously derived from other bodies of theory and from guesswork). In that sense, the resulting constructs represent a moment of 'provisional closure' within knowledge, open to further confirmation but also to falsification. In the Arts and Humanities, however, theory is often not directly underpinned by enquiry – in that sense, it is more a moment of 'openness' than of 'closure', a primarily *speculative* endeavour designed to lead to a debate maintained at the theoretical level rather than a systematic enquiry which is conventionally required to move 'down' to the level of evidence to secure itself as 'knowledge'. As the phenomena about which explanation is sought become less susceptible to any kind of controlled observation and measurement – such as is clearly the case in many areas of philosophy for example, but which is also true of areas of media and cultural inquiry – the idea of theory as a realm of *self-contained intellection* becomes more appropriate.

Many areas of media research have clearly had to confront the broadly 'scientific' and then more specifically 'social scientific' issues concerning the conditions of theoretical adequacy and the relationship (including the possible determinative effects) of theory upon methods and data. But media research, and particularly television studies, has been influenced by a strong 'philosophical' tradition too, coming through from critical social theory and, more recently, from the varieties of cultural theory. Some of this work has been pitched at the highest, most abstract of levels – it has been 'grand theory' (often variously Marxist, structuralist, psychoanalytic and postmodernist in derivation; see the account in Skinner, 1985). Moreover, the precise extent to which critical theory is interested in furthering an *understanding* of how things are as opposed to offering a generalized *critique* of how they are presumed to be has sometimes been difficult to gauge. Whatever might be judged of value by way of particular perceptions and insights, few academic endeavours can have worked with such sheer assertiveness, such an absence of conditionality on their discourse, as the varieties of critical theory. At least part of the allure for younger scholars, part of the 'glamour of theory', has lain precisely in the taking up of uncompromising 'positions' with such confidence and style.

During the 1980s, it was assumed by some that 'theory' was going to get to places which research could not reach (Thompson, 1978, remains a classic critique of the general tendency, despite its own specific intellectual moment and focus). 'Theory', refinable at the purely theoretical level, appeared simply to need careful *application* to instances. In this model, descent to the particular was more often 'illustrative' than it was 'investigative'. In part, such an emphasis was the product of resolute (and excessive) anti-empiricism, a rejection of the conceptual conservatism, and the accompanying political complicity, perceived in much social science.

FOUR TYPES OF THEORY ABOUT TELEVISION

Theories about television are, of course, informed by media theory more generally. They also display varying degrees of applicability to other media. But the specificity and impact of television as a *cultural* form has given its theoretical literature a distinctive character. For one thing it is far more informed by Arts and Humanities thinking, particularly by versions of the literary/philosophical tradition, than the broader range of work on 'media and society' or the earlier literature of academic commentary which was generated around the press and around advertising. I think that the theories which have been developed about television can usefully be divided into four types – theories of representation, theories of medium, theories of institution and theories of process. There are clearly other, useful ways of classifying theories, but this rather obvious typology helps in organising the kind of preliminary 'audit' I want to present here. In some theoretical work, these types either combine or, indeed, merge. In practice, rather than providing exclusive, self-consciously delimited foci of interest, they have formed the core for theoretical accounts which then frequently encompass other aspects of television, subsuming these as secondary to the main focus. This sometimes occurs as a process of totalisation from a quite narrow initial base.

A split which traverses all of them, though to different degrees, is one which I have commented on elsewhere (Corner, 1991) – that between a view of television as essentially an agency of public information and a view of it as essentially an agency of popular culture and popular entertainment. I want to look at each of my four types in turn before developing some points about their interconnection and the possibilities they offer for development.

Theories of Representation

In general, studies of television developing out of the tradition of mass communication research had a tendency to ignore the symbolic, textual complexity of television programmes and to emphasise, instead, the 'output' of 'content'. Such an approach inevitably resulted in a radically foreshortened view of television's character as a whole new system of socialised aesthetics, one in which quite unprecedented interconnections between 'the real' and 'the imaginary', between depiction and social subjectivity, were being established and in which the visual image was quickly becoming of momentous political and cultural importance.

In Britain, it was the influence of literary and film studies on the formation of interdisciplinary media studies in the early 1970s which provided a new emphasis on matters of representation, and then the structuralist/semiotic 'turn' within this which provided the primary framework for theory. The work of the University of Birmingham Centre for Contemporary Cultural Studies was of the most formative significance, particularly those working papers authored or co-authored by Stuart Hall (for instance, Hall, 1974) although Fiske and Hartley's *Reading Television* (1978), drawing on the Centre's work, made the 'cultural reading' of the television 'text' an accessible new critical practice in teaching. Within this strand of enquiry, theories of representation supported the more general, Marxist theory of ideology and ideological reproduction, particularly in the influential version provided by Althusser (1971) where, conceptualised in terms of a representational process involving both language and image, ideology becomes the key factor in the maintenance of Western political stability. A number of characteristics of television's dominant forms of social representation were seen to exemplify the features of ideological communication identified by Althusser – for instance, the 'interpellative' devices by which it engaged and addressed the attention of individuals-in-society and the kinds of 'misrecognition' of social relations which followed from the use of various means of displacement and mystification. Television's extensive use of the 'direct address' mode, its varieties of interrupted narrative, its range of 'realisms', dramatic and journalistic, often to provide illusory effects, took on a directly political impact within this perspective (see Corner, 1992).

The theoretical developments which followed closely paralleled the rise of Althusserian 'ideological critique' in literary studies and film studies, where an existing tradition of theory as critical speculation was combined with newer ideas of theory as the main dynamic of a materialist 'science' of society (a combination seen at its most confident in Eagleton, 1976). However, whereas literature was regarded by many Marxist critics as a form which itself frequently exposed the contradictions of ideology, a function in large measure of the 'critical creativity' of authorial transformation and of a subtle and deep textual structure, in general no kinds of television output were accorded such redeeming epistemological and aesthetic qualities. Later writers have sometimes revised this judgement but theories about the distinctive 'realist' efficiency of television in circulating distortive social imagery (of class, gender and race as well as of specific issues and events) continue to be dominant. These have produced a marked sense of television (particularly US television) as, representationally, a 'bad object'. This object routinely encourages, if it does not actually instil, 'bad' forms of subjectivity in viewers by mechanisms frequently conceptualised in terms of the subconscious, psychodynamic positioning which the viewing of dominant forms of television entails as well as in terms of content. Just how far this badness has been judged redeemable by better, more 'progressive' forms of representation and revised content has varied. Some theories have implied little scope for this, while others have turned on formal and thematic innovation and its possibilities. The question of 'redeemability' importantly figures in other types of account too, as I shall suggest below.

The notion of 'liveness' (an ontological feature often unusefully conflated with the stylistics of 'immediacy') has been a major component in theories of television representation. It has been either through real or pseudo liveness that many critics have seen the distinctive illusory or distortive potential of television to lie, engaging the spectator within the terms of an ontology which is extensively and successfully ideological in character (Feuer, 1983). The degree to which contemporary television even tries to project itself as 'live' is limited however, and a number of commentators (see Caldwell, 1995) have judged that an excessive concern with 'liveness' has been detrimental to theoretical development. It has led, in their view, to an ignoring both of the great variety of ways in which the recorded image is now used within dominant forms of television across all genres and of viewers' own understanding of the ontological status of what is seen on the screen.

The nature of television's specific forms of temporality, however, its organisation of'continuity' across interruption and widely diverse kinds of 'look' and 'sound' has been an important point of reference for those trying to address and theorise its particular representational system. Hall (1975) discussed both its distinctive mix of 'relay' and 'channel' functions (allowing both weak and strong kinds of mediation in relation to an anterior event) and Ellis (1982) influentially pointed to the 'segmental' character of studio-based construction, producing a temporality and a system of spatial and narrative development different from that of cinema, with its single camera shooting technique.

Productive for debate though such ideas have been, shifts both in technology and in aesthetics have radically undercut the capacity of such theories to speak to the full range of even mainstream broadcast output. A similar fate has befallen attempts at establishing theoretical work on genre (see Caughie, 1991 for an original and suggestive generic perspective). While some valuable analytic conceptualisation has been done on the modalities of representation (particularly of scopic field, spoken address and narrativisation) out of which television as a system of programmes is constructed (for instance, Wilson, 1993; Corner, l995a) the rate and diversity of development (and, increasingly, the rate of inter-generic hybridisation) has thwarted the emergence of anything like as relatively stable an ontological and aesthetic purchase on television as, for instance, has been provided for cinema. With such a varied, dispersed range of codings about which to be inclusive, theories have been forced so far 'up' from instances as to become virtually self-dissipating.

Over the last decade, television representation has been discussed extensively in terms of postmodernism (e.g. Fiske, 1991; Collins, 1992). When its centrality to modern popular culture is combined with its apparent capacity for generating 'simulacra' on a scale which blurs the distinction between reality and artifice and also with the high level of inter-textual referencing and stylistic eclecticism evident in some programming, this is not surprising. However, it has notably been specific kinds of television (e.g. the newer game shows, serial dramas, popular music programmes and channels) which have received most attention here (see Kaplan, 1987; Goodwin, 1993; Livingstone and Lunt, 1994). A whole range of popular output remains difficult, if not impossible, to fit within postmodernist criteria, despite strenuous attempts at inclusiveness. Given their scope (discussed further below) it is difficult to decide whether most postmodernist attempts at theorising television are usefully categorised as 'representational' in focus. However, changing aesthetic practices, and particularly changes in the nature and modes of circulation of imagery, have certainly been a key point of address in such theories, even if a connection with more general notions of 'medium' has been a significant feature too.

Representational theories have suffered from two kinds of limitation when they have been used to provide the core for comprehensive accounts of television. There has been the limitation described above – of achieving explanatory generalisation across an increasingly wide and changing range of forms. Even more importantly, there has been the limitation on accounts of 'influence', a limitation so strongly recognised in the last few years as to bring about a radical drop-off in theoretical discussion of representation and to cause a major realignment of theoretical interest, towards audience interpretation. I shall pick this point up more fully later, but I have noted how many representational theories, though focused on form, were also concerned with questions of influence (whether conceptualised as 'ideology', 'myth', 'ritual' or whatever). Indeed, some of the more politicised theories of representation were interested in form *only insofar* as it was a device of influence. The opening-up of the poststructuralist debate about the contingency of televisual meaning, about the pragmatics of understanding and significance, together with the empirical precedent of Morley's classic *Nationwide* study (Morley, 1980), put limits on this line of representational argument which still largely remain in place.

Theories of Medium

Theoretical interest in television as a medium is often hard to differentiate from an interest in representation. However, whereas the latter places emphasis on television's aesthetic, discursive character across the generic range (though usually with some emphasis on either its journalistic or its entertainment functions), the former works, right from the start, at a more general level. It addresses television as a cultural technology, the social influence of which is more a matter of its general properties as a technology than anything to do with particular conventions of programming or types of output (Meyrowitz, 1994, outlines these factors usefully). Marshall McLuhan was undoubtedly the most influential pioneer theorist of television as a medium (notably in McLuhan, 1964) and it is not surprising that a revival of interest in his works on the spatial, temporal and sensory aspects of television, often seen to be that of a postmodernist *avant la lettre*, has occurred. McLuhan's own thinking on these matters was greatly prompted by the earlier studies of Harold Innis on the macro-cultural changes brought about by communication technologies. Innis's writings (for example, Innis, 1951) though less fashionable than McLuhan's, are still an important source of 'medium' theory. It is important to note, though, just how tightly McLuhan's agenda is drawn around the abstracted relationships posed between technological characteristics and sense experience. Political, economic, sociological or even aesthetic questions hardly figure on it all, and although the stimulating character of his pithy overstatements cannot be denied, his influence on later scholars has often included a degree of de-politicising abstraction and the adoption of a 'techno-visionary' rhetoric.

A move away from representational theories of television towards 'medium' theories (not, however, as strong a shift as that towards processual ideas) has partly been the consequence of a gradual, selective movement in general theoretical activity from a (confidently) Marxist to a (nervously) postmodernist agenda. On this new agenda, the special capacities of television to transform spatial and temporal relations, to 'displace' many established forms of social experience, sometimes setting up parasocial substitutes (of a kind partly prefigured by Horton and Wohl, 1956) and to feed into that social and personal reflexivity and indeed anxiety which is often seen as a feature of late modern/postmodern society (as in Giddens, 1990) are important factors. The combination of centralised transmission with wide-ranging domestic reception provides the axis upon which this displacement effect can work, an effect which, in some accounts, is seen to be aided by the commodifying logics of the television industry. In the USA, the work of Joshua Meyrowitz (1985) on the effect exerted by television on traditional social and community life has received much attention, while a more self-consciously postmodern and politicised exploration of the culture of dislocation and displacement which television generates is given by Margaret Morse (1990). Morse's focus on the idea of 'everyday distraction' might be seen in part to indicate a concern with representation rather than medium, but it is to the general cultural and ontological consequences of the technology rather than to specific features of representational order that Morse is drawn. A parallel can be made here with the work of Raymond Williams and his widely-cited notion of 'flow' (Williams, 1974). 'Flow', as all good television students know, was the term used by Williams (writing after his experiences in the USA) to indicate the sequential, ongoing character of television programming, its impetus and continuity across the planned interruptions and insertions (e.g. commercials, embedded trailers) and across the repetitions and the shifts of item. Although 'flow' is not without its problems as an idea (see Dienst, 1994), Williams sees it as both a matter of organisation (it is 'planned') and as a matter of viewer experience. Like Morse's 'distraction', it is also judged negatively; its presence is viewed as further evidence of the bad cultural consequences of an increasingly commercialised television system, consequences which have more to do with the organisation of the medium itself than with specific representations. In fact, Morse's own account is centrally concerned with developing Williams's notion of 'mobile privatisation', a condition whose paradoxicality, spatial character and tension between public and private realms are seen to be sustained in large measure by television's 'medium' functions.

John Ellis, in putting forward the claim that television attracted the 'glance' of viewers rather than, as in cinema, their 'gaze' (Ellis,1982), offered another way of perceiving medium-effect relations. Here, what is seen as the essentially casual mode of viewing (partly a function of the technology itself and partly of the domestic contexts of attention, with their concurrent activities) is linked both to a reduced sense of TV's aesthetic value and, at the same time, a perception of its taken-for-granted (and therefore ideologically effective) permeation of the everyday. Many critics have since pointed to the unacceptability of such a generalisation of viewing levels, indicating the huge variation across genres and time of day as well as in specific domestic/personal contexts (Caldwell, 1995, brings this out well).

With the exception of McLuhan's essays and the work of Meyrowitz, most of these theories about television as a medium have tended to regard it *pathologically*, reconfiguring culture in unprogressive ways. Even Meyrowitz's optimism about new 'at-a-distance' relationships is tempered by ambivalence and occasional anxiety. Unlike theories concerning representation, the generalising drive of medium theories works against differentiation between channels, genres and programme formats, so that it is much harder within this framework even to begin to specify *where* change for the better might come from and *what* it might look like. At their worst, medium theorists can also slip into the technological determinism which always threatens an emphasis of this kind, 'bracketing out' from primary consideration both the specific communicative interface between programme and viewer and also specific institutional, economic and historical settings. However, medium theories, like theories of representation, vary considerably in the attention given to other factors, including to the political and economic elements of television as 'institution'. Silverstone (1994), for example, uses a 'medium' perspective in trying to connect with psychoanalytic accounts of self-development, with the nature of macro-cultural change in societies centred on consumption and with the literature of reception studies. The result, though provocatively eclectic, risks being too dispersed in its coordinates to develop much by way of explanatory leverage.

Theories of Institution

Theories of institution are primarily concerned with the organisational structure of television and the embedding of this within specific political and economic systems. Although they inevitably have a concern for what appears and what does not appear on the screen – without this, the significance of television and the importance of researching it would be hard to claim – they see neither the symbolic/expressive dimension nor the cultural–technological profile as warranting primary attention. It is the linkage of organisation (funding, production, distribution, regulation) with the activities of the state and/or with market structures which most requires conceptualisation. Although traditional mass communications research paid attention to organisational factors, at the level of theory it is the political economy strand, drawing on

Marxist accounts, which has been most active here (for recent exposition, see for instance Garnham, 1990; Murdock and Golding, 1991; Meehan et al., 1994).

British studies, focused on the tensions and growing contradictions of the 'Public Service' model of provision as it undergoes deregulation and privatisation, have differed in their concerns from North American work, which has had to engage with the reality of a much more intensively commercialised system right from the start.

It follows from the nature of institutional perspectives that they are likely to be much more alert to historical and national specificity than theories of 'representation' or of 'medium' since the institutionalisation of television often shows variety within national boundaries let alone across them. This fact introduces limits on the level of generality which theories of television as an institution can reach, although the taking of the instance of US network television as internationally generalisable from has often been one way in which these limits have been escaped, sometimes with distorting consequences. However, the more clearly that television is seen as placeable within the structures and flows of global capitalist accumulation as it adjusts its strategies for the commodification of time and leisure to a new era of telecommunication development, the more transnational the conceptualisation of it can become, despite the risks of abstraction beyond the levels of *explanatory* engagement.

A longstanding problem for political economic theories has been the predictability of given forms of television output (and thereby, if indirectly, of given 'effects') from the evidence of specific kinds of institutionalisation. In particular, the relationship between the commodity form which television takes and its political and cultural character as knowledge and entertainment is posed as an issue. It is hard to imagine any researcher arguing that no links exist – it is the *degree* of causality (for Marxist theories, producing a version of the classic arguments about economic determinism) which is in question. New developments in the television systems of post-Communist Europe as well as the deregulation and expansion of Western systems (particularly through satellite and cable and through convergence with IT systems) will provide fresh evidence by which to assess television as institution. This assessment will be in terms of variations in funding profile, regulatory regime, the organisation of production and distribution and then the impact of all these upon other factors (among the emerging assessments here, see Sparks, 1996). Such developments will also undoubtedly show a number of possible relationships, market-mediated or not, between the state, civil society and television systems (see the essays in Dahlgren and Sparks, 1991, and the discussion of television's 'public sphere' character in Dahlgren, 1995).

Although 'commodification' has been widely used as a term of self-sufficient critique, with the implication or sometimes the explicit suggestion that only 'decommodification' provides an acceptable alternative (see Keane, 1991), the number of *different ways* in which television programmes can have a commodity character and in which 'exchange value' can coexist with 'use value', require further attention. Practically, the real possibilities for television systems working free of commodity value are extremely limited and likely to become more so.

Theories of Process

'Process' is perhaps a more awkward category to use than the other three. Of course, all theorising about television *assumes* process, but many theories of the kind I have discussed earlier see it as *entailed* by, and *predictable* from, something else (e.g. representational form, cultural–technological character, institutional setting) rather than requiring exploration in its own terms, as a matter of variable relationships and contingencies. By theories of process I want to indicate those conceptualisations which *directly* confront relational issues, issues of interaction and interdependency, rather than working with assumptions about them. It follows that processual ideas will often have a more complex sense of causality than theories extrapolating from one privileged focus.

In discussing theories of representation above, I noted how there was a division between ideas of television as primarily an agency of public information and knowledge and ideas of it as an agency of popular culture and entertainment. This is also true of processual theories, in the one case leading to a concern with social cognition and the relation of information to power (e.g. Dahlgren, 1995) and in the other leading to questions about pleasure and imagination, with a more recent emphasis on sexuality and identity (e.g. Heide, 1995).

Another important split within processual perspectives is between attempts to conceptualise process primarily in relation to questions of 'production' and attempts to conceptualise it in relation to 'consumption'. Over the last ten years, an emphasis on questions of consumption has become dominant in media research, producing argument not only about the neglect of production but also about how best to theorise and research consumption practices (see for instance, the critical reviews in Morley, 1992; Robins, 1994). This shift partly reflects a broader, steady move away from (and sometimes against) those Marxist models, once so influential in the structuring of the field, which focused on the 'productionist' factors of economic determination and ideological reproduction. More narrowly, it reflects the route from 'text' to 'reader' taken by much work on programme form and content, particularly following the example of Morley (1980). Here, reception has been regarded as a constitutive moment of communication process, in a way which not only opens out on to variability but which also places limits on the kinds of explanatory conceptualisation that can be generated from consideration of pre-receptional moments alone, whether these be concerned with television as institution, medium or representational form. Using the cultural studies terms, this has been a move from 'encoding' and 'message structure' to 'decoding'. Within the cultural studies tradition, it has been accompanied by a gradual weakening of 'ideology' as the main processual term.

There is no doubt that the conceptualisation of power within a notion of televisual process has now become a matter of the utmost importance and difficulty in view of the range of qualifying factors, and the uncertainties about established concepts, which have been introduced into research and debate. Just how to relate viewing behaviours and practices, variously conceived, to power is the nub of the issue (for an illuminating dispute on this, one which also connects with fundamental divisions over methodological perspective, see Rosengren, 1996 and Jensen, 1996). In my view, a reengagement with 'production' – institutional structures, institutional settings and specific production relations – must be part of any development here. Studies of institutions and of production which themselves engaged more closely with representation and/or consumption could make a significant contribution. For instance, on television news, Schlesinger (1978), Ericson et al., (1987) and, most recently, Jacobs (1996), indicate a developing strand of workplace ethnographies which open up a broader theoretical agenda about the construction of public knowledge. For television fiction, Jostein Gripsrud's recent study of *Dynasty* (Gripsrud, 1995) attempts a major multi-aspectual analysis by keeping its substantive focus tight. What seems absolutely clear is that many studies of media consumption (including many reception studies), although their origins may lie in 'processual' thinking, have sometimes worked within a very non-processual conceptual framework. Closure around, and then total-isation from, 'viewers' meanings' or a postmodern and rather miasmic notion of the 'everyday', has simply replaced the older closures and totalisations around 'text', 'medium' or 'institution'. Exploration of the changing public and private spheres which television now sustains needs a far less exclusive agenda.

THEORETICAL DEVELOPMENT AND TELEVISION RESEARCH

I remarked earlier how the extent to which theorisation of television is seen as a matter of *ideas for debate* rather than as the *formulation of explanations in relation to prospective or collected evidence* varies. A 'theory' about television's role in providing temporal coherence within every-day life may be so general as to be incapable of direct empirical testing, it can only be subject to debate in terms of conceptual criteria and its 'fit' with other ideas, some of which may have an evidential basis. A 'theory' about image–text relations in a new kind of music programme will be subject to critical argument – insofar as reference to the details of the programme may serve to question or, indeed, in the case of inac-curacies of observation, completely to refute such a theory (the extent to which textual criticism is a form of empirical enquiry, albeit one which is often procedurally loose, often goes overlooked). A 'theory' about the social class base of variations in audience response to a political broadcast is immediately open to direct empirical testing if it is a hypothesis and to empirical challenge if it is derived from a programme of study.

The search for explanatory accounts and relationships of the broadest possible kind is clearly a major part of academic investigation. In pursuit of this, work at the theoretical level must both lead substantive inquiry and also be informed by it; it must serve both as a moment of opening and speculation and of attempted consolidation and closure.

It must, inter alia, work at a number of levels and orient itself both towards other, alternative and perhaps conflicting, conceptualisations (by modes of critique and of adaptive use) as well as towards phenomena.

However, I think that general recognition of differences between *kinds of theory* about television (in terms of level, scope, derivation and conditions of adequacy) needs to be much clearer and more explicit than it often has been. A stronger and more explicit sense of the *accountability of theory* should complement this and might act as a check against the tendency towards exclusive totalisation and premature generality which the field still displays. The debates generated by the new anti-foundationalism may well indicate modified terms for pre-scribing such accountability but they do not displace the need for it (see the instructive comments on this and related themes in Seidman and Wagner, 1992).

My comments are not intended to suggest the desirability of bringing theoretical work on television within one, unifying discourse of endeavour. The different conceptual frameworks which researchers use will ensure the continuation of mismatches and conflicts between what 'television' is perceived to be as an object of research. The humanities and social sciences will continue to support distinctly different modes of engagement and analysis (often making usages like 'television studies' and, even more so, 'television theory', extremely awkward – see Corner, 1995b).

Despite its hectic recent history as a site for high theoretical adven-ture, it is unlikely that any new 'grand theories' will emerge which can be used to provide a totalising framing for television study in the future. Middle-range, analytic concepts, developed 'downwards' from a broad range of political and social ideas and developed 'upwards' from substantive analysis are likely to prove the most productive route for development. A more thorough engagement with the spectrum of thinking about public life and cultural form taking place in the humanities and social sciences (e.g. in economics, anthropology, social psychology and political science) is crucial to progress here. Theory about television, though it will often, inevitably, use a specialist register for debate and critique, cannot be self-contained in its principal categories – it is a subset of social and cultural theory and needs always to con-ceptualise television within these wider parameters while retaining an interest in specificity. In a complementary way, it needs always to address television within the wider, substantive settings of economy, society and culture too (in different ways and to different degrees according to the specific theoretical project).

In the broad terms I have outlined, it will be increasingly difficult for any significant theoretical work on television *not* to have a strongly 'processual' character, although that does not mean that representational, medium and institutional foci cannot usefully be retained. By giving a certain emphasis to theories of process here I am not so much offering a category of 'solution' to the problems raised by other theories as indicating the category within which I think most new problems will arise. What aspect of television a given line of theoretical inquiry focuses on, what it chiefly tries to explain, what it finds most significant and what relationships it poses as important will continue to be matters of choice. What horizontal and vertical relationships it recognises, the dependency and the status of its claims-making in relation to evidence and counter-evidence, the way in which it proposes itself for development by way of refinement, testing, application etc. are matters about which tighter conventions of practice might be encouraged. This is true both of perspectives from social studies and those of a more literary/philosophical origin.

In study of television, internationally, there is some indication of a move to ideas which more firmly engage with substantive factors, have a more precise perception of inter-relational complexity and carry a stronger sense of their own theoretical positioning and its possible limitations and foreshortenings.

If such a move can begin to encourage stronger linkage between the levels of conceptualisation and of investigation and between the different sub-areas of study, then it will be good news indeed. Theoretical purchase on the condition and consequences of 'television' in society (and therefore our capacity to be cogently and effectively critical about its various dimensions) will develop rather than disperse or, as it has sometimes looked likely to recently, collapse.

ACKNOWLEDGEMENT

I would like to thank Kay Richardson and Philip Schlesinger for their detailed comments on an earlier draft.

NOTE

Since this article was accepted for publication I have read with interest the essays in Bordwell and Carroll (eds), 1996 on the intellectual reconstruction of Film Studies following years of doctrinal rigidity. In line with my own arguments here, they emphasise a theoretical endeavour in which the connection with empirical work is strong and the development of 'middle-range' concepts an important goal.

REFERENCES

Althusser, L. (1971)'Ideology and the State', pp. 123–73 in *Lenin and Philosophy and Other Essays*. London: New Left Books.

Bordwell, D. and N. Carroll (eds) 1996: *Post-theory: Reconstructing Film Studies*. Madison: University of Wisconsin Press.

Caldwell, J. (1995) *Televisuality*. New Brunswick, NJ: Rutgers University Press.

Caughie, J. (1991)'Adorno's Reproach: Repetition, Difference and Television Genre', *Screen* 32(2): 127–53.

Collins, J. (1992)'Television and Postmodernism', pp. 327–49 in R. Allen (ed.) *Channels of Discourse Reassembled*. London: Routledge.

Corner, J. (1991) 'Meaning, Genre and Context: The Problematics of"Public Knowledge"in the New Audience Research', pp. 267–84 in J. Curran and M. Gurevitch (eds) *Mass Media and Society*. London: Edward Arnold.

Corner, J. (1992) 'Presumption as Theory: "Realism" in Television Studies', *Screen* 33(1): 97–102.

Corner, J. (1995a) *Television Form and Public Address*. London: Edward Arnold.

Corner, J. (1995b)'Media Studies and the"Knowledge Problem"', *Screen* 36(2): 147–55.

Dahlgren, P. (1995) *Television and The Public Sphere*. London: Sage.

Dahlgren, P. and C. Sparks (eds) (1991) *Communication and Citizenship*. London: Routledge.

Dienst, M. (1994) *Still Life in Real Time: Theory After Television*. London/Durham, NC: Duke University Press.

Eagleton, T. (1976) *Criticism and Ideology*. London: Verso.

Ellis, J. (1982) *Visible Fictions*. London: Routledge.

Ericson, R., P. Baranek and J. Chan (1987) *Visualising Deviance*. Milton Keynes: Open University Press

Feuer, J. (1983) 'The Concept of"Live Television": Ontology as Ideology', in E. A. Kaplan (ed.) *Regarding Television*. Los Angeles: American Film Institute/University Publications of America.

Fiske, J. (1991)'Postmodernism and Television', pp. 55–67 in J. Curran and M. Gurevitch (eds) *Mass Media and Society*. London: Edward Arnold.

Fiske, J. and J. Hartley (1978). *Reading Television*. London: Methuen.

Fornäs, J. (1995) *Cultural Theory and Late Modernity*. London: Sage.

Garnham, N. (1990) *Capitalism and Communications: Global Culture and The Economics of Information*. London: Sage.

Giddens, A. (1990) *The Consequences of Modernity*. Cambridge: Polity Press.

Goodwin, A. (1993) *Dancing in The Distraction Factory*. London: Routledge.

Gripsrud, J. (1995) *The Dynasty Years: Hollywood Television and Critical Media Studies*. London: Routledge.

Hall, S. (1974) 'Encoding and Decoding in the TV Discourse', Stencilled Paper Seven. Birmingham: University of Birmingham CCCS.

Hall, S. (1975) 'Television as a Medium and Its Relation to Culture', Stencilled Working Paper. Birmingham: University of Birmingham CCCS.

Heide, M. (1995) *Television Culture and Women's Lives: 'Thirtysomething' and the Contradictions of Gender*. Philadelphia: University of Pennsylvania Press.

Horton, D. and R. Wohl (1956) 'Mass Communication as Para-Social Interaction: Observations on Intimacy at a Distance', in *Psychiatry* 19: 215–29. Reprinted in J. Corner and J. Hawthorn (eds) *Communication Studies* (4th edn). London: Edward Arnold.

Innis, H. (1951) *The Bias of Communication*. Toronto: Toronto University Press.

Jacobs, R. (1996) 'Producing the News, Producing the Crisis: Narrativity, Television and News Work', *Media, Culture & Society* 18(3): 373–97.

Jensen, K. B. (1996) 'The Empire's Last Stand: Reply to Rosengren', *European Journal of Communication* 11(2): 261–7.

Kaplan, A. (1987) *Rock Around the Clock*. London: Methuen.

Keane, J. (1991) *The Media and Democracy*. Cambridge: Polity Press.

Livingstone, S. and P. Lunt (1994) *Talk on Television*. London: Routledge.

McLuhan, M. (1964) *Understanding Media*. New York: McGraw Hill.

Meehan, E., V. Mosco and J. Wasko (1994) 'Rethinking Political Economy: Change and Continuity', pp. 347–58 in M. Levy and M. Gurevitch (eds) *Defining Media Studies*. Oxford and New York: Oxford University Press.

Meyrowitz, J. (1985) *No Sense of Place: The Impact of Electronic Media on Social Behaviour*. New York: Oxford University Press.

Meyrowitz, J. (1994) 'Medium Theory', pp. 50–77 in D. Crowley and D. Mitchell (eds) *Communication Theory Today*. Cambridge: Polity Press.

Morley, D. (1980) *The 'Nationwide' Audience*. London: British Film Institute.

Morley, D. (1992) *Television Audiences and Cultural Studies*. London: Routledge.

Morse, M. (1990) 'An Ontology of Everyday Distraction', pp. 193–221 in P. Mellencamp (ed.) *Logics of Television*. London: British Film Institute.

Murdock, G. and P. Golding (1991) 'Culture, Communications, and Political Economy', pp. 15–32 in J. Curran and M. Gurevitch (eds) *Mass Media and Society*. London: Edward Arnold.

Robins, K. (1994) 'Forces of Consumption', in *Media, Culture & Society* 16(3): 449–68.

Rosengren, K. E. (1996) Review article (K. B. Jensen's *The Social Semiotics of Mass Communication*, Sage 1995), *European Journal of Communication* 11(1): 129–41.

Schlesinger, P. (1978) *Putting Reality Together*. London: Constable.

Seidman, S. and D. Wagner (eds) (1992) *Postmodernism and Social Theory*. Oxford: Blackwell.

Silverstone, R. (1994) *Television and Everyday Life*. London: Routledge.

Skinner, Q. (1985) *The Return of Grand Theory in The Human Sciences*. Cambridge: Cambridge University Press.

Sparks, C. (1996) 'Post-Communist Media in Transition', pp. 96–122 in J. Corner, P. Schlesinger and R. Silverstone (eds) *International Media Research: A Critical Survey*. London: Routledge.

Thompson, E. P. (1978) *The Poverty of Theory and Other Essays*. London: Merlin.

Williams, R. (1974) *Television, Technology and Cultural Form*. London: Fontana.

Wilson, T. (1993) *Watching Television*. Cambridge: Polity Press.

Chapter 10

MEDIA STUDIES AND
THE 'KNOWLEDGE PROBLEM'

———⊃⊂———

In the mid-1990s, review of the condition of Media Studies, both as a teaching and a research area, seemed to me to be prompted not only by the further development and visibility of the field as many more courses were started and related publications proliferated, but also by the rise of the new 'audit culture' in Higher Education. As teaching and research across the range of disciplines became subject to proce-dures of 'quality' assessment and grading, the question of the identity and aims of Media Studies was raised more often. In addition, the issue of the vocational aspect of study became increasingly controversial. Many of the points raised in this short essay I have developed further in my introductory chapter. Although it ran the risk of offending people working in the area, often teaching and researching within terms not of their own making, the piece received a generally positive response as opening up a more focused debate about the field and its future.

I want to suggest that both teaching and research in Media Studies have a 'knowledge problem' which has recently become more visible and troublesome as a result of uncertainties, tensions and regroupings in the area. All fields of study have knowledge problems of course, and although they vary in the amount of self-consciousness they display about them and their degree of engagement with them, there has been a broad shift towards paying them more attention and making such attention an explicit and central part of study discourse.

167

Knowledge problems concern what it is that academic inquiries seek to find out, and the kinds and quality of data and of explanatory relations which particular ideas and methods might be expected to produce. In response to them, disciplines not only engage more closely and innovatively with questions of conceptualisation and technique, but also develop a reflexive, sceptical sense of their own knowledge production and its vulnerabilities. From some perspectives, this sense may be considered radical, in that those who have it are placed in the position of professional doubters rather than practitioners in relation to the disciplinary project. One effect of the sweep of postmodernist thinking in the humanities and social sciences has undoubtedly been to encourage this latter tendency.

The distinctive character of the problem – or better, the set of problems – which confronts Media Studies is due partly to the history of this field, partly to the very diverse nature of its object of study, and partly to the particularly ambitious form of interdisciplinarity to which this diversity tends to lead. I am talking primarily about upper case 'Media Studies', a singular noun designating an institutionalised, self-conscious grouping, rather than lower case 'media studies' (studies of the media), a plural designation referencing a broader range of work distributed across humanities, social science and even technological fields.

Media Studies needs to engage with expressive form, social action and social structure. It needs to explore the political and psychological determinants and consequences of media processes, as well as their discursive and technological means. To do this, it necessarily either draws on directly, or else 'shadows' with varying degrees of explicitness, concepts and methods developed in the primary disciplines. How far does it thus constitute itself as a unified project of inquiry? Or how far does it become an *aggregation* of inquiries, which are placed into tighter or looser relationships of contiguity with each other and have greater or lesser levels of mutual awareness and tolerance? If the latter were the case, one would expect the knowledge problems themselves to be an aggregation of the problems confronted by the constitutive disciplines. They would not therefore be addressable at a general level since the field would have no general discourse of inquiry within whose terms it could consider itself. But without such a discourse, what constitutes 'core knowledge' in the area for the purposes of teaching and research training programmes? Such a question has become a very real one for many course planners and others active in institutionalising (and, indeed, variously assessing) Media Studies.

The particular academic configuration of British Media Studies today is primarily the product of two things. First of all, a certain combination of arts and social science approaches to the analysis of the media, institutionalised in the design and teaching of the interdisciplinary Communication Studies courses of the 1970s. Secondly, the legacy of Structuralist Marxism. North American, Australian, other European and Scandinavian versions of Media Studies vary in the resemblance they bear to this formative mix, but the relationships and interconnections are never quite the same.

The arts and social science combination in Media Studies is essentially one which brings together 'criticism' and 'sociology' as modes of academic knowing. Criticism is a mode privileging *individual percipience*, in which knowledge is the product of sustained analytic attention and intellection. It has a direct, informing link with 'opinion' and, indeed, it is 'opinion' rather than 'theory' as such which is its main generator of ideas. That such opinion is, by definition, subjective (often deeply and self-declaredly so) is by no means a drawback to the larger project of intercritical activity (characterised as 'debate'). In literary studies, for instance, a powerfully rendered account of a major novelist may be prized for its 'originality', precisely for the way in which it differs from the interpretations made by other people. In order for it to be acclaimed thus, it is necessary for some assumptions to be made about what is 'there' to be the object of such 'insight', yet this does not mean that the new interpretation has then to be established as dominant in relation to others. Critical knowledge does not contain truth claims requiring supersession or even superordination of this kind.

Sociology, on the other hand, in its classic and defining empirical project, is essentially a mode privileging *method*. However cautiously it relates itself to (or distances itself from) natural science paradigms, the production of knowledge is normatively regulated by the use of procedures which are explicit, in line with intersubjective agreements on validity (even if these are only partial) and able to be replicated by those who wish to 'test' findings. What the procedures produce is, first of all, 'data', and then an analysis and explanation of this data. Both data and the analyses which are made of it (the two should not be confused) have a very different status from 'criticism'. It can be recognised, without thereby succumbing to positivism, that data carries claims to objectivity, however much these claims are qualified by recognition of both the imprecision of the research tools and the constructional dimension of the research concepts themselves. Analytical constructs used in asking questions of data and in attempting to answer them have objectivity obligations as a consequence, however tentative and conditional the honouring of these may be. *Theories*, here, are mostly explanatory propositions, with considerable attention being paid to those which are open to forms of empirical testing and, then, to the bodies of analysed evidence which result.

It is part of the intellectual history of Media Studies in Britain that it was formed, not only out of an increasing recognition of the media's political and cultural significance, but out of a dissatisfaction with both the perceived inability of literary-style analyses of the media to go beyond their textualist boundaries, and the perceived inability of conventional social science to engage with the complexity of meaning-making forms. The most influential perspective for this formation was Cultural Studies, the history of which has recently received a good deal of attention, at the same time as the field of study which is covered by the term has become increasingly subject to institutional variation and plain opportunism.[1] Initially an attempt to push out English Studies (meaning and value) to the point where an interconnection with the Sociology of Culture (structure and practice) could be established, Cultural Studies was soon displaying increased autonomy as an academic (but, at this stage, exclusively research-related) project. The warrant for this autonomy came neither from literary analysis nor social science. It was taken primarily from Structuralist Marxism, with the Althusserian perspective on ideology and the social formation as its 'sociology', and semiotics (taken largely from Barthes and Eco) as its 'criticism'. In relation to this broad framing, Film Studies continued to exist and develop, deriving much of its own identity from its earlier literary and art historical connections. In some institutions this was extended to become Film and Television Studies in a manner which usually (and not unproblematically) continued to privilege the Film Study agenda. The broadest, and perhaps earliest, grouping for undergraduate work was Communication Studies, which often had a strong Cultural Studies element and a core of media work, but which also tended to draw on a wider range of arts and social science perspectives on communication, including those from psychology. The rapid development of Communication Studies in the mid 1970s was in part prompted by the need for polytechnics to design attractive interdisciplinary courses which could draw on a considerable range of staff interests. Alongside these interrelated projects, there remained a Sociology of Mass Communications (updated as Media Sociology), which was still the dominant category by which the systematic study of the media had an *international* identity.[2] Moreover, despite the growth in Cultural Studies approaches, some of the best research work done in the 1970s was done from within one version or another of a sociological problematic, though very few of the researchers were at that time involved in the construction of a field at undergraduate level.[3]

If the most significant question for any academic venture concerns the kind of things it wants to find out, then the Media Studies produced within the framework of Cultural Studies worked with an exceptional directness of purpose. It wanted to find out how the media worked to achieve an effective level of ideological closure on contemporary consciousness in a situation of capitalist development where direct control at the point of production and/or consumption was admitted to be far from total. This was its defining problematic, and engagement with it (initially brilliantly suggestive but, one might argue, increasingly prone to repetition and self-confirmation) produced a strongly theoretical–critical discourse linked to a subtle, typologically elaborate scheme for investigating textuality.[4] The conventional body of social scientific analysis was often deemed to be unsuitable for the new task, being irredeemably flawed both in aims and methods. A conflation of 'empiricism' with 'empirical' too frequently provided the project with that *Other* against which it defined itself epistemologically and politically, reinforcing the tendency to circular reasoning. This did not stop substantial internal rifting on questions of theorisation however, quite apart from sustained and cogent criticism from researchers whose own application of Marxism suggested the need for primary attention to be given to the 'political economy' of the media and who strongly contested the increasingly hermetic terms of Cultural Studies' attention to ideology.[5]

The knowledge problems affecting current Media Studies have therefore to be understood, first of all as ones relating to a non-unified field in which the very different modes of criticism and sociology have been brought together but, in general, *not integrated*. Indeed, it might be said that in many studies and on many syllabuses they have not yet fully come to terms with each other. Secondly, they have to be understood in relation to a formative period of development which was dominated by debates centred on a Marxist-structuralist paradigm, in which a comprehensive materialist account of media power, independent of non-Marxist modes of study, was seen not only to be in the offing but, indeed, to be already under refinement.

Perhaps more than any other area of institutionalised inquiry, this foundational version of Media Studies has, in effect, been left marooned within the new post-Marxist, post-Structuralist context for political and social debate. One has to be careful with the inflections of 'post' here. It is not useful to talk of 'the collapse of Marxism' in a way which primarily refers to the dissolution of Communist Eastern Europe but which then smuggles in assumptions about the 'collapse' of Marxist theory and analysis. Nevertheless, materialist theory itself has had to adapt (sometimes quite radically) to changed historical circumstances and to an intellectual context increasingly aggressive towards it. Even the terms of the Political Economy perspective, robustly historical and empirical though they were, have received adjustment and may well receive more.[6] Theories of ideology have virtually disappeared from the media research agenda altogether, though not from the undergraduate syllabus, where their gloomy diagnoses are sometimes to be found in bizarre combination with the cheerful populism which has become a more recent perspectival option.

An often ambivalent, running engagement with postmodernism has provided Media Studies with one avenue for the continuation, beyond Structuralist Marxism, of a semi-autonomous (and self-defining) critical discourse. However, there has been a discernible shift away from unifying high theory, a shift which has revealed more strongly the character of Media Studies as a divided field, running an arts and social science project together in ways which are often uneasy. No longer able to afford itself the luxury of devising its problems to fit already available solutions, it has been returned to a re-engagement with those discipline-based knowledge problems from which it once aspired to autonomy. Nowhere is this more true than in the rise of ethnography (both pro-ductional and consumptional) as a mode of media inquiry. Although an element in early Cultural Studies, it was only in the mid-1980s that ethnography started to become a defining approach, displacing textual analysis in research if not in teaching. Ethnography initially promised a way of looking at ideological reproduction 'from the sharp end',[7] but it quite quickly modulated into being the methodological correlative of a more general shift from a primary concern with researching 'power' to either an emphasis on 'resistance' or an expanded, contextualising interest in the way in which media meanings are articulated within the terms of the 'everyday', the multiple lifeworlds of society. As researchers soon became aware, whilst it could be innovatively applied to the researching of media meanings, ethnographic inquiry carried with it a long history of methodological debate, both in sociology and anthropology. Indeed, many of the inquiries into audience interpretation which have been undertaken in the last decade are radically *mis*described as 'ethnography', since their relationship to researched subjects and to data is often very different from that of the broader tradition.[8] These inquiries often (and justifiably) have a particularity of research focus around mediated meanings which makes them, by comparison, 'narrow' and even 'shallow' in their specifically ethnographical engagement.

Ethnographic work has typically run into two related kinds of problem as an academic project. It can slip into *descriptivism*, rendering ever thicker accounts of process but being unable to make any clear connection upwards to explanation because of a gravitational commitment to ground-level phenomena. It can also suffer from an *empiricism* whereby this commitment makes it lose sight of its own constructed, authorial character. In recent work, a third problem can be discerned – largely a product of postmodernist influence. This is an over-correction of empiricism where the self-consciousness of the researcher is raised to the point at which interest in the researcher-method-subject relationship begins to displace interest in the researched subject itself. The first and the third of these tendencies are now discernible within the new media ethnography.

Put simply, then, a post-Marxist Media Studies has been substantially shorn of those intellectual features which gave the field a degree of unity. It has been returned to a multiple knowledge problematic which draws extensively on the problems of established disciplines and then adds to them issues of combination and adaptation. Its general theories of ideological function, and the contexts of social formation and historical trajectory within which these were set, have been exposed to radical doubt (the recent upsurge of interest in the ideas of Anthony Giddens, whose conceptualisations of structure and agency have been receiving intensive debate in Sociology for well over a decade, is just one sign of current theoretical reorientation).[9] The mode of textual analysis around which a large part of the field organised itself – semiotics – has received a general theoretical questioning as well as increasingly being seen to fail in generating significant and original substantive analyses. The push out to 'ethnography', while it has produced some excellent work, is in grave danger of running into the doldrums as theoretical uncertainties reduce the consequentiality of its data or it becomes obsessed with its own authorialism.

There is yet another factor, an 'opportunity' carrying the possibility of 'threat', currently determining the shape of work under the Media Studies heading. This is the pull of vocationalism.[10] It would be hard to deny the mutual benefits of establishing a connection between study of the media and the acquisition of practitioner/professional skills. Many institutions have put considerable effort into making these connections work at the level of student experience. But too often, despite the claims about integration and complementarity in course documents, there has emerged the strongly dualistic language of 'theory' and 'practice', a language in which the whole project of academic inquiry is radically misdescribed as 'theory' and thereby pre-packaged for *potential* marginalisation as a form of complementary study. For if invited to allocate priorities between 'theory' and 'practice' in an educational world of increasing competition and scarce resources, what manager would not find the eminent soundness of the latter more attractive than the ethereal, not to say self-indulgent, ring of the former? To put it this way is to caricature the present situation, but many Media Studies departments could testify to the way in which what looked to be a splendid partnership between academia and the 'real world' can, when aided by certain committee decisions and nervousness over revenue, quite quickly turn into a relationship of domination, affecting resources, appointments, course development and careers. The emerging recipes for the expedient combination of academic and vocational goals will clearly exert a considerable influence on the mid-1990s identity of the area.

Such a view of Media Studies, facing a new and risky future situated rather uncertainly on the fringes of the social sciences (unlike Film Studies, it cannot situate itself primarily as an 'arts' project without a potentially fatal degree of contraction) might provoke several objections. Among these, it might be argued that the shaping influence of feminism and postmodernism upon the post-Marxist character of the field needs more attention.

Feminism has contributed important new ideas to the study of media processes, particularly to an understanding of the relationships between textuality and subjectivity. It has also produced an impressive range of new knowledge about the media and has considerably raised awareness of gender inequalities at all levels of the mediation process.[11] It is arguable, however, whether it has introduced wholly new *ways* of conducting research. Its conceptual and methodological innovations (and its valuable critique of existing practice) do not, on their own, seem to provide the basis for an adequate, 'internal' reconstruction of the field.

Postmodernism has become a quite central factor within the terms of much recent media analysis, but its weirdly dual status as both a *condition* to be debated (present or not? good or bad?) and as a *perspective* for reflecting on and analysing conditions, has made its influence more a matter of climactic change than intellectual renewal. It is tempting to regard 'it' (the singular entity is presumptuous) as being as much a symptom of current cultural shifts and intellectual blockages as a means of engaging with them.

Do the scale and complexity of these knowledge problems suggest that it would be best for the area to disaggregate itself into separate discipline interests? No. As a collective grouping for teaching and research activity around one of the major defining components of modern life, the category of Media Studies continues to be a valuable one. There is also a great deal of good and interesting work being done under the heading (certainly as much as, if not more than, within any other academic grouping of equivalent size) though it is being done from a range of different disciplinary backgrounds, using different concepts and methods and applying sometimes entirely different criteria about permissible forms of argument, about what constitutes 'evidence' and about the conventions for connecting propositions to data. In these circumstances, we need fewer rhetorical attempts at unification and at separate intellectual identity and a wider recognition of the lack of perspectival and methodological autonomy from the mainstream of international social studies which a post-Marxist Media Studies can show. This means, among other things, recognising a wider range of productive contexts for researching those questions of power, representation and subjectivity/identity which were so high on the 'autonomous' agenda although not always satisfactorily investigated within its terms. It means a re-engagement with general social theory and also a re-engagement with social research method at every point where the project seeks to produce something other than a discourse of 'criticism' (which it should also continue to do, exploring questions of form, value and response, whilst being very aware of what it is doing). It is important to note that these are not in any way conservative recommendations, fitting study of the media back, after a period of eclectic adventures, into the traditional and worthy frameworks of the disciplines. For it is clear that these frameworks and their associated methods have been fundamentally challenged at a number of points (by feminist research and by concepts of cultural process among other factors) and that hardly any social studies field has remained free of introspection, debate and change. But the project of social studies inquiry has not, as some would have it, collapsed into futility or terminal self-doubt, nor has it become indistinguishable from the various perspectives and procedures of the arts and humanities. Research on media and ideas about media processes need to be centrally introduced into its remaking and into its critical engagement with contemporary modernity.

In any reassessment of Media Studies, the question of how to think beyond 'ideology' is worth a measure of separate consideration. On its pivotal importance to the field as initially constituted (and therefore on the size of the hole its waning now leaves), I am fully with Christopher Williams in his recent attempt at a critical stock-taking.[12]

Williams wonders if it is not 'the case that ideology has become a hopelessly unusable term?' and finds that, indeed, 'repeated wielding of the clumsy club' has had a widespread deleterious influence.[13] Offering a more positive view of the future, he notes that it needs to be 'replaced' and, with quite extraordinary optimism, that 'this replacement need not, I think, be too difficult'.[14] In fact, what Williams subsequently says shows the sense of brisk remedy to be deceptive. First of all, he suggests that the concept of 'ideology' can be broadly equated with the idea of the 'social', but this would seem to be true of only the most loose and totemic of usages and hardly offers adequate 'replacement'. More indicatively, he goes on to suggest a wide variety of different conceptual alternatives, each relevant to different areas of inquiry, thus abandoning his idea of 'replacement' altogether since it was precisely the job of 'ideology' to unify ideas about meaning and power across the full range of expressive forms. Is there not more which needs rescuing from the debates about 'ideology' than Williams suggests? What the term points to is the way in which the legitimation of economic and political interests interconnects with the making of public meanings, often by way of the naturalisation of the contingent. The focus on the links between representation and power, between the aesthetics and logics of signification and the forcefields of value and disposition within which subjectivities are developed, seems well worth maintaining, albeit in rethought terms. No shift to 'opinion' or 'attitude' or, following Williams' concern with textual form, to 'diction', 'expression' or 'convention' will keep a tight enough hold on the factors which need to be addressed *in their interarticulation*. Open argument about these issues, particularly as they appear (or not!) in a range of current research contexts is now, I agree with Williams, one of the most pressing requirements.

Media Studies is still a new arrival within the institutionalised orders of academic inquiry. Its house-style of boldness and disrespect, its eclecticism and its conceptualising zeal have brought dividends in the context of the older, often evaluatively conservative, disciplines. But as many of these disciplines rethink themselves in the 1990s, the same qualities could quite easily work against its possibilities for steady self-assessment and for theoretical and methodological reconstruction as, precisely, a *multi*-disciplinary field of social research. Since the variety, intensity and importance of the media industries and their activities continue to increase, this would be both an academic and a political loss.

NOTES

1. The major surveys include Graeme Turner, *British Cultural Studies: An Introduction* (London: Unwin Hyman, 1990): Patrick Bratlinger, *Crusoe's Footprint* (London: Routledge, 1990): and Jim McGuigan, *Cultural Populism* (London: Routledge, 1992).

2. A history of interrelated institutional and research developments in the late 1970s, particularly those relating to the course validations of the Council for National Academic Awards, would be useful. I merely offer a background sketch here. See also Alan Durant, 'Noises offscreen: could a crisis of confidence be good for media studies?', *Screen* vol. 32, no. 4 (1991), pp. 407–28.
3. Apart from the continuing work of an older generation of social scientists, including Jay Blumler, Denis McQuail, Jeremy Tunstall and James Halloran, there was the work, among others, of Philip Schlesinger, Michael Tracey, Philip Elliott, Peter Golding and Graham Murdock.
4. Here, Hall's stencilled papers from the Birmingham Centre for Contemporary Cultural Studies were the single most influential publications, and often more theoretically cautious than selective quotation of the key formulations might suggest.
5. Graham Murdock and Peter Golding at the Leicester Centre for Mass Communication Research were chiefly identified with this position, following their article 'For a political economy of mass communications' in R. Miliband and J. Saville (eds), *The Socialist Register 1973* (London: Merlin, 1973). As the Cultural Studies perspective increased in influence through the mid-1970s, the terms of their critique became stronger.
6. The continuing case for 'Political Economy' is updated in Peter Golding and Graham Murdock, 'Culture, communications and political economy' in J. Curran and M. Gurevitch, (eds), *Mass Media and Society* (London: Arnold, 1991). See also Nicholas Gamham, *Capitalism and Communications* (London: Sage, 1990), particularly his introductory essay, which as well as reflecting on recent theoretical developments also argues against those tendencies which 'cut the field off from the main stream of social science' (p. 2).
7. David Morley seems to have been the first to use the idea of 'ethnography' as an indication of the *kind* of approach required, in his highly original CCCS stencilled paper 'Reconceptualising the media audience' (1974).
8. These issues have been brought out more fully in Virginia Nightingale, 'What's ethnographic about ethnographic audience research?', *Australian Journal of Communication* no. 16 (1969), pp. 50–63.
9. Giddens' ideas figure strongly in Graham Murdock's recent and useful survey of the media and modernity in 'Communications and the constitution of modernity', *Media, Culture and Society*, vol. 15, no. 4 (1993), pp. 521–39.
10. This is commented on in Durant: 'Could a crisis of confidence be good for media studies?'. Durant's polemical discussion engages with many important points concerning the development of media education,

doing so from a position often close to the one I am outlining here. His own answer to his title question is 'yes, it could'.

11. See, for instance, the excellent appraisals in Liesbet van Zoonen, *Feminist Media Studies* (London: Sage, 1994).

12. Christopher Williams, 'After the classic, the classical and ideology: the differences of realism', *Screen* vol. 35, no. 3 (1994), pp. 275–92. Williams sets out by appearing to take issue with an earlier piece of mine, but his only substantial complaint seems to be that I do not go as far as he would wish in my questioning of 1970s theory. See John Corner, 'Presumption as theory: "realism" in television studies', *Screen* vol. 33, no. 1 (1992), pp. 97–102.

13. Williams, 'After the classic, the classical and ideology', p. 276.

14. Williams, 'After the classic, the classical and ideology', p. 287.

INDEX